WE LOVE YOU BRUINS

WE LOVE YOU BRUINS

BY JOHN DEVANEY

Boston's Gashouse Gang
From Eddie Shore
To Bobby Orr

SPORT
MAGAZINE
PRESS

ACKNOWLEDGEMENTS

I am indebted for the many ways Herb Ralby helped in obtaining the basic materials for this book. Boston sports columnist Harold Kaese contributed material on the early days of the Bruins. And articles in SPORT Magazine written by Al Silverman, Ed Fitzgerald, Lee Greene and Stan Fischler were also of great help. My thanks, too, to Bill Kipouras of the Boston Herald-Traveler for his zealous fact-checking.

First published in 1972 by the SPORT MAGAZINE PRESS
205 East 42nd Street, New York, New York 10017

Library of Congress catalog card number: 71-180525
International Standard Book Number: 0-87794-031-2

Printed in U.S.A.

For my father, who would have been a Bruin fan, I am sure, if the boat from Ireland had docked in Boston.

CONTENTS

Chapter I
WE LOVE YOU, BRUINS

Phil Esposito skates across the mouth of the cage, collects the short pass and *whap!* He slaps the puck by goalie Glenn Hall and into the corner of the cage.

It is a meaningless goal in a meaningless game: the 1970–71 Bruins have already clinched first place in the Eastern Division of the National Hockey League. But it is Phil Esposito's 75th goal in a season in which he and his Bruins teammates have smashed some 40 NHL scoring records. And now the capacity crowd in Boston Garden is up and cheering, not for this goal, but for all the goals and all the records set by this record-breaking crew this season. The cheering goes on ... and on ... and on ... For an incredible two minutes these Boston fans stand and cheer, their roars telling Espy and Bobby and all this team just how much these fans think of them and what they have accomplished.

Now it is a few weeks later, playoff time in Boston, a Sunday afternoon in April, a dank and cloudy day. ZERO HOUR FOR B'S AT 2 P.M., a headline proclaims. Indeed it is a zero hour. There will be no tomorrow for either the Bruins or the Montreal Canadiens: this is the seventh and final game of the opening round of the Stanley Cup playoffs. One team will win, the other must go home and dream of what might have been.

Boston scores early in the game on a hard shot by Ken Hodge. Then the Canadiens rally, Frank Mahovlich and Rejean Houle scoring to put them ahead, 2–1. Early in the third period they boost that lead to 4–1. Now the Bruins fight back, trying to come from behind as they have so often in the past. Johnny Bucyk backhands a shot by Canadien goalie Ken Dryden, the score is 4–2, and here come the Bruins.

They lash shot after shot at Dryden, Phil Esposito alone whacking 11 line drives at him during this game. But now the kid goalie seems as impregnable as a stone wall, knocking down shots with his stick, kicking away screamers with an acrobat's grace. Here comes Espy one last time, driving straight on Dryden, no more than 20 feet away, whacking the puck straight at the cage. But Dryden flashes out a glove and snares the puck. Espy sums up the frustration of these Bruins—and their fans—by angrily swinging his stick, as though he were hitting a baseball, against the glass partition. Minutes later the game ends, the Canadiens the 4–2 winners. The Bruins skate slowly off the ice, their fans trudging out of the Garden into the gloom of Causeway Street.

Those two games symbolized the 1970–71 season for the Boston Bruins. There were those electrifying highs as the Great Boston Scoring Machine smashed record after record. And there were those disappointing lows as the team came close to setting a home winning streak—and failed—then went into a Stanley Cup playoff—and failed.

Moments at the heights, moments at the bottom. This has been true of the Boston Bruins since they played their first game in 1924. They lost that game and they were way down at the bottom of the league that season. But they rose to the top within five years to win the Stanley Cup. In the 1930s, the 1940s and the 1950s they were at or near the top most every season. During most of the 1960s they were at or near the bottom. But they came back in 1970 to win another Stanley Cup, the fourth of their proud history.

The Bruins have always come back, which may be one reason why the fans, the devoted, loving fans, have made the team perhaps the most loved of all the sport's teams. On banners in the Garden, on hundreds of thousands of bumper stickers throughout New England, in the millions of words spoken and written by their fans from Providence to Bangor, this is the hard-core message: *We love you, Bruins!*

There is another message that passed unspoken between the Bruins and their fans as the 1971–72 season began. It is unspoken because these Bruins and their fans know it does not have to be said. But if you talk to Bruins like Bobby Orr, as I did in the hours and days and weeks after that heart-ache of an April Sunday afternoon in Boston, the message comes across clear and ringing: *The Bruins will come back!*

This is a book about the Bruins of yesterday and the Bruins of today. It is the story of the legendary Bruins, now enshrined in Hockey's Hall of Fame: Bruins like Eddie Shore and Milt Schmidt, Dit Clapper and Frank (Mr. Zero) Brimsek. It is also the story of Bruins who will never be forgotten by the fans who saw them play: Mel (Sudden Death) Hill, the hero of the Bruins' dramatic overtime triumphs as they won the 1939 Stanley Cup; the Kraut line wingmen of the 1930s, Bobby Bauer and Woody Dumart, and their teammates Roy Conacher and Bill Cowley; the Uke Line of the 1950s and early 1960s, Bronco Horvath, Vic Stasiuk and Johnny Bucyk, the Chief, Johnny Bucyk, still with the Bruins, and the greatest scorer of all time for Boston. Finally this book will look at Bobby Orr, at Phil Esposito, and all the Bruins of today.

The Boston Bruins were born in the imaginative and keen

mind of Charles F. Adams, a Boston retail store owner and
amateur hockey fan. The first Bruin team skated onto the ice
for the 1924–25 season, becoming the first U.S. team to play
in the league. That Bruin team, made up mostly of former
amateur hockey players, won only six games. Determined to
bring the Stanley Cup to Boston, Charles F. Adams purchased the stars of an entire minor hockey league, the Pacific
Coast League, to get the one player he needed: Eddie Shore.

Eddie Shore, the Edmonton Express, was the first Big Bad
Bruin. Rampaging down the ice and knocking over opponents in his bull-like charges at the nets, he led the 1928–29
team to the Bruins' first Stanley Cup victory in their first
season in the newly-built Boston Garden.

In the mid-1930s the Kraut Line—Schmidt and Dumart
and Bauer—came to Boston to become the spearhead of one
of the greatest of all hockey teams, perhaps the greatest. That
team finished first in four straight seasons—1937–38 to 1940–
41. In two of those four years the Bruins won the Stanley Cup.

World War II broke up that team, the Krauts enlisting as
a unit in the Royal Canadian Air Force. In the 1940s and
1950s the Bruins were nearly always contenders but never
winners. Then came those losing years of the 1960s until Orr,
Espy and the rest brought the Stanley Cup back to Boston
after 29 years of waiting and praying. And then 1970–71:
the season in which the Bruins finished first, the champions of
the Eastern Division. This was the team that won more
games than any team in NHL history – the Great Boston
Scoring Machine.

Chapter II

THE GREAT BOSTON SCORING MACHINE

The Bruins. The Big Bad Bruins. The 1970–71 Big Bad Bruins.

This was the team that set some 40 National Hockey League records. This was the team that scored more goals in one season than any team in history—399. This was the team that won more games in one season than any team in NHL history—57.

And on and on … the most home victories in one season: 33. The most road victories in one season: 24. The most short-handed goals in one season: 25. The most assists in one season: 695. The most scoring points in one season: 1,093. The most 20-goal scorers in one season—10 of them. And how the old Boston Garden rocked with the roaring for those 10 names: Esposito, Orr, Bucyk, Hodge, Cashman, Stanfield, Sanderson, Westfall, McKenzie, Carleton.

Great names in Boston, the names that helped bring the Stanley Cup back to Boston after a painfully long wait of 29 years. There had been those losing years of the Sixties, the team stuck at the bottom of the league for eight frustrating seasons.

Then Bobby Orr came out of junior hockey, everyone predicting he would lead the Bruins out of the wilderness. And the 18-year-old Bobby, a Nureyev on skates, did lead them out, teaming with that bunch from Chicago—Phil Esposito, Fred Stanfield, Ken Hodge—and another kid, that long-maned street brawler, Derek Sanderson. Battling with them were the old bunch, the guys who had suffered through the thin years—Terrible Teddy Green, Johnny Bucyk, Ed Johnston, Eddie Westfall and company.

The Bruins rose from last place in 1966–67 to third place in the East in 1967–68. But in the opening round of the playoffs the Canadiens blew them out in four straight games. The Bruins roared back the next season to finish second in the East. And in the playoffs this time it was the Bruins who did the blowing, knocking out the Toronto Maple Leafs in four straight games, scoring 24 goals and yielding only 5. In the semi-final round the Bruins took on the Canadiens, who were on their way to a second-straight Stanley Cup triumph. The Bruins battled with the Canadiens through several overtime games, outscored them 16–15 in the series, but bowed after six games, four games to two.

In the 1969–70 season the Bruins went all the way, fulfilling a prophecy made three years earlier by Phil Esposito. They won 40 games and lost only 17 to finish second in the East. In the opening round of the playoffs they faced off against the New York Rangers. After the first four games the series was tied, two games apiece.

The Bruins would not lose another game in this 1969–70 season. They raced by New York, four games to two. They wrecked Chicago in four straight. And they won the Stanley Cup by beating St. Louis in four straight, Bobby Orr turning Boston into a Bedlam when he whisked a shot through goalie

Glenn Hall's legs in overtime of the fourth game for the 4–3 game-winner.

Minutes later Bruin veteran Johnny Bucyk was skating around the Garden rink, the Stanley Cup cradled in his arms, the huge crowd roaring its joy at seeing the proud Bruins once again the champions of professional hockey. When President Nixon came to Boston he knew at one glance the sentiments of this city, the fans flaunting a huge banner that proclaimed: THE BRUINS ARE NO. 1.

The next season, 1970–71, was the year of The Great Boston Scoring Machine. Phil Esposito, that Roman-nosed warrior, led all the scorers with more points (152) and more goals (76) in one season than any man in the history of pro hockey. Right behind him, the No. 2 scorer in the league, was the blond Bobby Orr, who scored more goals (37) in one season than any defenseman ever, and who collected more assists (102) than anybody ever—period.

The records of those 1970–71 Bruins run on and on.

Most three-goal games in one season—7 (Phil Esposito)

Most points in one season by a defenseman—139 (Bobby Orr)

Most goals in one season by a center—76 (Phil Esposito)

Most assists in one season by a leftwinger—65 (Johnny Bucyk)

Most assists in one season by a rightwinger—62 (Ken Hodge)

Most points in one season by a center—152 (Phil Esposito)

Most points in one season by a leftwinger—116 (Johnny Bucyk)

Most points in one season by a rightwinger—105 (Ken Hodge)

Most power-play goals in one season—25 (Phil Esposito)

Most goals by a line in one season—140 (Esposito 76, Hodge 43, Cashman 21)

Most points by a line in one season—336 (Esposito 152,

Hodge 105, Cashman 79)

Most game-winning goals in one season—16 (Phil Esposito)

There were moments in that astounding 1970–71 season that can never be put down in a record book. Some will be etched in the memories of those who saw them long after the team's 1970–71 records have been broken.

There was Teddy Green on his night, standing at center-ice in the Garden, head bowed, hiding his wet eyes, as the capacity crowd poured down its emotions on him, applause swelling over the arena for this tough man who had come back from a skull fracture that had almost killed him. And his wife coming out onto the ice, escorted by Johnny Bucyk, tears streaming down her face. People standing, applauding, happy, and crying in their happiness.

Then, too, in Boston Garden—all season long—there were the crashing sounds of the Big Bad Bruin Symphony, the thudding sounds of bodies being whammed against the boards—thump! thump! thump!—and then, suddenly, unpredictably, a fight, a brawl, the crowd up and screaming, sensing blood.

There was the wild night of November 8, 1970. Derek (Turk) Sanderson engages the Canadiens' Phil Roberto and knocks him down. Roberto leaps up, fists flying, the two men flailing at each other in front of, then on the Canadien bench. Excited Bruin fans, fearful that the Canadien players will gang up on Turk, jump atop the Canadiens. The Canadiens lash back and now there is a writhing mass of players and fans battling behind the Montreal bench.

Later Sanderson said he wound up near (and on) the Montreal bench trying "to get" Canadiens' coach Claude Ruel, but Ruel had *fled* down an aisle leading outside the stadium. According to Sanderson, when the brawl broke out, Ruel was yelling, "Get the bad guy, get the bad guy," meaning Sanderson. "He's always yapped at me, ever since I can remember," the Turk said. "But he beat it in a hurry."

As far back as Eddie Shore—and as recently as 1970 when Bobby Orr and the other Bruins joked about the unwillingness of some players to take the puck against Boston—the Bruins have been the Big Bad Bruins, wearing down opponents by physically punishing them. But last season they were not *always* physical. "We're the Big Good Bruins," Bobby Orr said late in the season. Coach Tom Johnson explained what Bobby meant. "We play the game any way the other team wants. You want finesse, we'll give you finesse. You want a rough game, we'll give you a rough game."

Employing that combination of finesse and roughness, the 1970–71 Bruins won more games than any team in the history of the NHL. They won as a team, but each player—and coach Tom Johnson—contributed his individual skills and personality to give the team its record-breaking success as well as its character. To understand how and why this team was so successful, you must look at its individuals—who they are, what they are like, and how they got to be the way they are.

You must meet the Bruins.

Chapter III

BOBBY ORR:
"He Has No Fear"

Bobby Orr walked slowly across the living-room. He stared out the window, looking down from his high-rise apartment in Boston at the stream of afternoon traffic along the roadway bordering the Charles River. He was thinking about Deanne Deleidi, the young woman who comes to the Bruin games in a wheelchair and who must go home each night to an iron lung. The world is full of people who haven't been lucky, he thought, like these kids who would be coming to the apartment this afternoon, these young kids, not even 15 yet, who were dope addicts.

He turned to look at the oval table in the dining room, laden with ginger ale, Coke, potato chips. Once a week he invited a different group of young addicts to come to the apartment, brought here by a dedicated school teacher. The teacher had told Bobby that if he talked to the kids, he could help them to stop using drugs. So far the teacher had been right. There was one group of eight boys and girls who'd come here a month ago. Not one had gotten into trouble since, and that was unusual. These boys and girls mugged people in the streets, broke into houses, stole from stores to get money to buy drugs.

Bobby, turning back to the window, remembered one boy who had said to him, "Please help us." Bobby recalled saying to someone: "How ironic it is that these kids can talk to a stranger, but they can't talk to their own parents. But there's no communication in the family."

He glanced downward at the bustling streets around the Prudential Center. How many people were out there alone and scared and unable to communicate with those they loved. Athletes could help them, Bobby believed. Athletes, he'd been telling people, should get more involved in trying to help people with drug problems. "They'll listen to a player," he had told other hockey players, "where they might not listen to anyone else."

The buzzer sounded. These were the kids arriving now with Mrs. Janice Barrett, the teacher. Bobby went to the door to open it, a smile on his long face.

No one ever came to this game of hockey with more natural gifts than Robert Gordon Orr. Of the thousands of words that have been written about the invincibility of Orr, these three sentences, uttered by former Bruin coach Harry Sinden, perhaps best sum up the essence of Bobby Orr:

"Bobby Hull goes at top speed but he doesn't do everything. Gordie Howe does everything but not at top speed. Bobby Orr is really the first hockey player I've seen who does everything at top speed."

Once Sinden noticed that Orr's shots were rising too high. He suggested to Bobby that he try a different stick.

"That's not it at all," Orr said. "I'm not following through low enough. I'll start working on it."

"He was only 21 and he knew all about it," Sinden said later. "And his coach didn't. What I'm trying to say is that in those areas where he's weak, he knows it himself and he knows what to do about it."

The 5-foot-11, 180-pound Orr, who has the gangling look of a college shortstop, basically plays a basketball give-and-go game with the puck. He comes across the blue line with the puck, gives it off to a teammate, and then with his eye-dazzling swiftness and deking, as the players say, he darts past an opponent and, as often as not, is free for the return pass and a shot on goal.

It is a shot he can take from either the right or left side. Of all the players in hockey today, only one other—Gordie Howe—can shoot from both sides. And in the entire 55-year history of the NHL, no other defenseman has been a switch-hitter—not even the legendary Eddie Shore.

Defensemen, of course, are on ice primarily to stop goals and not to score them. While Bobby Orr can score goals himself and pass to teammates for other goals with the skill of a centerman—he also excels at stopping goals. And the way he stops them sometimes makes the other Bruins wince. (It is one measure of Bobby's greatness that when he is on ice, at least half the players on the benches are watching him.)

"If Bobby has a problem," Bruin goalie Gerry Cheevers once said, "it's just that he has no fear. No fear whatever. If nothing else will do, I swear he'll use his head to block a shot. He's already been hurt bad, and he'll keep on getting hurt. But that's his style. He won't change. He won't play it safe."

Indeed, writer Stan Fischler once saw Bobby use his head to block a shot, pay the price in blood and come back to show he was willing to do it again. In a game against Montreal Orr dove to block a shot and the whizzing puck ripped a jagged hole an inch above his right eye. Five stitches knitted together the hole; but the next morning the eye was

Tiny Thompson: No. 1 in a long line of stalwart Bruin goalies.

a purplish ball and shut tight.

That night the Bruins were again playing Montreal. "I feel bad," Orr told Fischler. "I wish there was no game. But it's a funny thing. Sometimes you play your best on days like this."

Early in the game Jacques Lemaire skated toward the net and shot. Again Bobby dived for the puck, but this time it struck his leg and bounced aside.

Bobby went on skating, one-eyed. Jean Beliveau took the puck and skated down the side of the rink. Orr crashed into him, slamming the taller and heavier Beliveau against the boards. Orr grinned and skated away. "There is," one NHL referee has said of Orr, "that streak of meanness in him that all the great ones must have."

Early in the third period the score was tied, 4–4. Bobby collected the puck in his own ice and burst up-ice. Two Montreal forwards, Henri Richard and Bobby Rousseau, cut across to intercept him but Bobby outsped them. A Montreal defenseman, Ted Harris, came up to meet him, looking to plaster him against the boards. But Orr feinted and Harris, going for the fake, brushed by Orr, who kept right on coming.

He sped at the Montreal goal from the right side, circled the net and came around the left side. Out of that one seeing eye he spotted a crack, maybe five inches wide, between the goalie's skate and the iron goalpost. Bobby crammed the puck through the gap and as he saw the black puck hit the nets he flung his right hand high into the air.

The crowd roaring, Turk Sanderson turned to Dallas Smith and said, "That kid ain't human."

Indeed, the way he plays both ends of the rink, he does seem superhuman. When the Bruins push the puck into the other team's ice, Orr comes up to guard the point. But unlike most defensemen, he does not always stay at the point, "If he has the puck at the point," a Bruin once told writer Jack

Olsen, "and somebody takes a run at him, that's the end. He'll give them that one-two-circle dance of his, that ballerina twirl, and he's moving in on the net at top speed. No other defenseman would dare do this, because meanwhile he's leaving the whole wing wide open. But I've never seen him get caught."

For a defenseman to be one-two in scoring for two straight seasons (Bobby was the scoring leader in 69–70 and second in 70–71) seems unthinkable. It would be akin to Dick Butkus leading the NFL in touchdowns or Juan Marichal leading baseball in home runs. In the entire history of the National Hockey League, going all the way back to 1917, only one defenseman has led the league in scoring—and that was Bobby Orr in 69–70. Bobby scored 33 goals and had 87 assists for 120 points—only the fourth player in history to score more than 100 points. And his assists were the most by any player ever, forward or defenseman. The next season, 1970–71, he was second in scoring only to Phil Esposito, and Espy had to set an NHL scoring record—152 points—to beat Orr's 139. But Orr had more assists than Espy, 102, and that was a record, breaking his own record of 87.

Bobby's achievements have won him more awards in hockey today than anyone except the veteran Gordie Howe. He has won:

The Calder Trophy as the Outstanding Rookie of 1966–67.

The Norris Trophy as the Outstanding Defenseman of 1967–68.

The Norris Trophy as the Outstanding Defenseman of 1968–69.

The Norris Trophy as the Outstanding Defenseman of 1969–70.

The Hart Trophy as the Most Valuable Player of 1969–70.

The Art Ross Trophy as the Leading Scorer of 1969–70.

The Conn Smythe Trophy as the outstanding player in the 1969–70 Stanley Cup playoffs.

The Hart Trophy as the Most Valuable Player of 1970–71.

The Norris Trophy (his fourth straight) as the Outstanding Defenseman of 1970–71.

Before Orr only Doug Harvey had won four straight Norris trophies (Harvey won seven altogether). Of all the defensemen in NHL history, only Eddie Shore won the Most Valuable Player award more than once. At 24, after only five NHL seasons, Orr has won two MVP awards and a total of nine major awards. By comparison, Gordie Howe, at 43 and after 25 NHL seasons, has won 13 major awards. Almost certainly Bobby Orr one day will own more awards than Howe.

Almost certainly. *Not* certainly. There is an Achilles heel in all of us, a vulnerable point. In Bobby Orr the vulnerable point is a left knee that has been carved open by surgeons and repaired. In the relentless savagery of the game of hockey, which has no room for pity, opponents often whack at the knee with their sticks. One day the knee could buckle—and a career suddenly end.

Ask Bobby about the knee and he smiles and say it's fine. But in moodier moments he admits to worry. "Maybe I don't show it," he has said, "but I worry. About my health, my legs. Lately I've been throwing up. The doctors say it's just nerves. I've been getting worked up too much."

"You mean," a friend asked, "they're all expecting too much from you?"

"There are people who say I'm not worth so much money. You get it a lot of ways . . . I used to have a brush cut but I let my hair grow. Now some people bug me about getting a haircut. But you've got to take the bad with the good."

Certainly many of the good things have come Bobby's way. During the past three seasons he has earned $400,000 in hockey salary, the most ever paid to a hockey player. In 1966 Orr, who had not played a minute of NHL hockey, signed a two-year contract for $65,000. That was far more money than most veterans were being paid; the average salary of NHL players was less than $15,000 a year. Immediately, stars like Hull and Howe demanded more money. When they got more the lesser players got more. So Orr, and his brilliant adviser, Alan Eagleson, raised the salaries of all hockey players—a bit of history that delights Bobby. He was even more delighted after he signed his latest contract in August of 1971. It called for $200,000 a year for five years—a $1 million contract.

These are all numbers to Bobby, much to Eagleson's dismay. "All this is going on around him," Eagleson once told writer Jack Olsen, "and he doesn't give a damn. He'll think nothing of carrying $20,000 worth of checks for five months. He gave me a check last June that he'd had in his wallet since January. It was for $11,000.

"He is entirely unmotivated by any personal desire for money. If he doesn't want to do something, he won't do it, no matter how much money is being offered. I have him on an allowance of about $20,000 a year, and he kicks back maybe half of it unused. He makes a quarter-million a year *off* the ice—endorsements and private deals and things—and I'm not saying how much on the ice. He'll be a millionaire in a few years, and he couldn't care less.

"I think one reason for this is that a part of him doesn't want to have this kind of money because it sets him apart from his teammates and that's the one thing he hates the most in the world. That's the one thing he'll fight you about, if you set him up as something apart from the team. He's the best team-man there ever was."

Bobby Orr, however, does care about money: He likes to give it away. "He's a bleeding heart and a do-gooder," Alan Eagleson says, exasperation in his voice. "And most of it is private. He doesn't even tell me about it. He doesn't get receipts and we lose all kinds of tax deductions because he doesn't make a record of it. Every once in a while he cleans out his whole wardrobe and gives it to a priest over at the Sacred Heart in Watertown. No, Bobby's no Catholic. He's barely even a Baptist. But he's the most Christian man I've ever known. He'll get $500 for an appearance somewhere and he'll give it to the first charity worker he sees. I asked him what happened to his bonus check last year. He says, 'Oh, I remember. I endorsed it over to Father Chase.' You wouldn't have space to list the things he's honorary chairman of: Muscular Dystrophy Association of Canada, United Fund of Boston, March of Dimes, all kind of things. But that isn't where his time goes. His time goes in visiting hospitals, orphan homes, poor kids, things like that. It's more than duty with him. It's an obsession."

You drive north to understand how Bobby Orr became the man he is. You drive 150 miles north of Toronto to the small resort town of Parry Sound, sitting on the edge of Georgian Bay, an outlet of Lake Huron. In mid-winter the temperature plunges to 30 below zero in Parry Sound, six-foot banks of snow lining the roads. Etched against the whiteness of the winter is a long black trestle, a relic of an old lumbering mill that dominates the town, stretching across the Seguin River.

Some 6,000 people live in Parry Sound during the winter. In the summers as many as 30,000 visitors flood into the town to bask in the sun and splash in the lake. Some of these visitors meet Arva Orr, Bobby's mother, who occasionally works as a part-time waitress in the coffee shop of one of the town's motor inns.

Doug Orr, Bobby's father, is a tall man nearing 50; he looks younger and resembles actor William Holden. He works at Parry Sound's only factory, Canadian Industries, which makes explosives. In 1942, when Doug Orr was 18, a Boston Bruins' scout came to Parry Sound and offered him a contract. Doug Orr was that good a hockey player. But Doug went off to help fight a war. He was a sailor on one of the Royal Canadian Navy's corvettes, guarding convoys on the perilous North Atlantic run.

Both Doug and Arva Orr go on working because they are the independent kind; they have refused to touch any of Bobby's money. But Bobby would not let them say no when he insisted they move from their drafty stucco house on Great North Road to a large new house, and some people around Parry Sound say it cost Bobby $100,000. All Bobby will say is, "I owe them more than I can ever give them back. They raised me right."

Bobby was born in Parry Sound on March 20, 1948. In the summers Bobby and his four brothers and sisters often went fishing with their father. When Bobby was only 9, though small and thin, he was playing hockey with his father and other grown men on the frozen Seguin River. At 12 Bobby played bantam hockey against bigger boys who towered over him: he stood only 5-foot-2 and weighed 110 pounds. But Bobby, the quick and evasive skater and stick-handler, was the team's standout on defense and its high scorer—even then.

His scoring helped Parry Sound to qualify for the Ontario Bantam Championship at Ganonoque. Parry Sound went to the final round with Bobby playing 60 minutes of hockey each game. In the final game the tiny 12-year-old Bobby would have played 60 minutes but he had to sit out two minutes because of a penalty. Parry Sound lost, 1–0.

At the tournament was a group of Boston Bruin officials. They had driven over from nearby Toronto, where the Bruins were playing, to watch two boys who had been recommended to them by scouts. Watching were Weston W. Adams, the club president; general manager Lester Patrick; coach Milt Schmidt; and then-scout Wren Blair.

"I'm watching the two kids," Blair recalls. "A funny thing happens. I see this little guy on the Parry Sound team out of the corner of my eye. It seems I'm going back to him all the time."

"I'll never forget it," Milt Schmidt says. "Bobby was about 5-foot-1 or so and his pants were so big they hung below his knees. Still, he was in complete control of the game."

The Bruins' officials forgot about the two kids they had come to see. After the game they talked about Bobby Orr. Maybe he was too small now, but, hell, he was only 12 and he would grow. Adams and Patrick decided they had to get Orr.

Their attack began immediately with a donation of $1,000 a year to support Parry Sound Bantam hockey. After two years of talking, an agreement was made: for a package of $2,700 that included new stucco for the Orr house, a $900 used car for Doug and a $1,000 cash bonus. Bobby—then only 14, mind you, and small for his age—would play for the Bruins' Oshawa farm team in the Ontario Junior "A" Hockey Association.

When little Bobby reported to Oshawa, a roll call was held, each player calling out his name and position. It came around to Bobby and the 14-year-old, surrounded by 18-year-olds, squeaked, "Bobby Orr, defense." Everyone roared. He looked like an underweight water boy. He certainly didn't look like a defenseman.

But he was. In his second season he scored 34 goals—a league record. Emile Francis, now general manager of the Rangers, saw him at Oshawa. "The kids would give him the puck," Emile says, "and then they'd stand around and watch him."

At 16, growing taller and stronger now, he was featured on the cover of MacLean's, the national Canadian magazine. Wren Blair was his coach at Oshawa and he kept reminding Bobby not to let all the publicity go to his head.

"I try not to read about myself," Bobby told a friend. "So

many people have been telling me not to get swell-headed I am scared to read anything about me."

After four years at Oshawa Bobby came up to the big league. The old pros were waiting to test this high-salaried whiz. "Don't back up," Wren Blair told Bobby. "Throw off your gloves and go at them."

Early in his rookie season Bobby was assaulted by Montreal's Ted Harris, one of the best punchers in the league. Bobby threw off his gloves and knocked down Harris. Harris got up. Bobby knocked him down again.

Later a grinning Orr said, "It's amazing what you can do when you're scared." But around the NHL the word spread quickly: this rookie was for real.

At first the fancy-skating, graceful Bobby made the other Bruins seem plodding. But then Bobby, Phil Esposito, Derek Sanderson and all the rest came together to lead the Bruins to the 1969–70 Stanley Cup. And no one who saw the final game of that Stanley Cup series will ever forget the shot that won the Cup for the Bruins.

The Bruins led the St. Louis Blues, three games to none. But the feisty Blues weren't quitting, and the fourth game went into overtime, tied 3–3. With some 30 seconds gone in the overtime, Orr was circling near the blue line when he saw the puck pop out from a group of players near the cage. He dashed for the puck, fielded it, then passed it to Turk Sanderson near the net. On the give-and-go, Bobby drove for the net and took the return pass from Sanderson. He saw that goalie Glenn Hall had slid toward the left post to guard against a shot by Sanderson.

"He'll be moving across toward the right side," Orr thought quickly, and he shot the puck straight on, figuring Hall would be in motion. The puck sailed between Hall's legs and snapped the rear nets. As it did Bobby was tripped by Blues' defenseman Noel Picard. But even as he sailed through the air, belly-down to the ice, an exultant smile lit his face. "I thought I was going to fly right out of the building," Bobby said later, "but I was so happy I didn't care."

One night, sipping beer with a friend, Bobby was talking about himself and his career. "OK, I'm lucky, right?" he said "I've been gifted, right? But the world is full of people who've not been gifted. Not only haven't they been gifted, but have had things taken away from them. All I have to do is see one of them—some little girl who can't walk and yet she keeps on smiling at me . . . All I have to do is see someone like that and then I don't think I'm such a big hero anymore. I think that compared to those people I'm a very small article. A very small article. It knocks me down pretty bloody fast. It cuts deep into me, and I'd rather not talk about it. It's very personal with me."

But there is one thing that the gifted Bobby Orr can't do. He can not—no way, no how—make a very small article out of Robert Gordon Orr.

Chapter IV

PHIL ESPOSITO
"ARMS AND LEGS AND 12–FEET WIDE"

This was a cool, fall afternoon in London, Ontario, the northerly wind flapping the topcoats of the Boston Bruin players as they sauntered out of the rink, laughing, tossing taunts and insults at each other. Two of the Bruins paired off and headed for a nearby pub. One was the veteran defenseman, Ted Green, the other a newcomer to the Bruins for this 1967–68 season: the tall, hulking Phil Esposito.

For three full seasons Phil had played for a winning club—the Chicago Black Hawks. Playing center on a line with Bobby Hull, Phil fed hockey's Golden Boy so well that Hull set a scoring record in 1965–66 with 97 points. But Chicago coach Billy Reay growled when Phil failed to score a point in the 1966–67 Stanley Cup playoffs. There was talk around the Hawks that Phil was too lackadaisical in practice, that he wasn't aggressive enough, that he tightened up in the big games.

In truth, Phil didn't skate into the playoffs with all the zest in the world. "I've lost a lot of confidence here," he told a friend one day. "They want a quick skater like Stan Mikita who'll run all over the place hitting guys. That's not my game. I'm the big, slower center but I think I'll get more goals and set up wingmen for goals by slowing things down out there."

Billy Reay didn't agree, and he sent Phil to Boston for one of those quick-skaters he liked, Pit Martin, as part of a multi-player deal. Now Phil was walking down a street at the Bruin training site in London, headed toward a favorite pub with Ted Green. Right from the start Phil had fitted in well with this Bruin team. When he arrived in London, the coach, Harry Sinden, presented him with an "A," and being an assistant captain made Phil feel a responsibility to the team that he had never felt with the Black Hawks.

Phil and Ted Green entered the swinging doors of the pub, found a table, and ordered two beers. When the beers came, Phil took a quick swig, the cold brew wetting a throat parched by practice. He set down the glass, thinking about that practice session. He'd noticed something, something he had never seen with the Hawks. He looked at Ted and wondered whether Ted had seen it, too.

"Greenie," he said, "do you think that there is a losing attitude here?"

The slit-eyed Green stared at Phil. "What the hell do you think?" Greenie roared. "How can you blame them after eight years of losing?"

Eight long years of losing. The Bruins had missed only seven Stanley Cup playoffs from their origin in 1924 to 1959. But from 1959–60 to the 1966–67 season, they had failed to make eight straight playoffs.

Quietly, Phil Esposito and Ted Green finished their beers. During the next few days Phil talked to some of the other players, telling them he thought this team could be a winner.

Someone suggested all the players get together and talk about the team. A meeting was called, players only, at the pub.

Each of the Bruins came to the meeting. Each stood up and said something about how they should all work together. Phil's turn came. He got up slowly from the table, his burly 6-foot, 200-pound body as menacing as a prizefighter's. He looked slowly around the room. "I think we got a team that can win," he roared at the players. "And if there is any ———here who thinks we can't win, then he doesn't belong on this———team."

A few weeks later, after the season had started, Phil took coach Harry Sinden aside one night in a jet airliner, the team flying back to Boston after a game in Montreal. "We played real good hockey tonight, Harry," Phil told the coach. "It will take us three years, but we are going to win the Stanley Cup."

That season, 1967–68, the Bruins rose to third, losing in the playoffs to Montreal in the opening round. The next year they finished second, going as far as the semi-final round before losing to the Canadiens in six games. In 1969–70, Phil's third year as a Bruin, the team did what he had predicted it would do: It won the Stanley Cup.

When Bobby Orr came to the Bruins in 1966, Bruin fans had begun to hope that the days of losing were near an end. But if you talk to hockey players, they will tell you that Bobby Orr would not have led the Bruins to the winning of the Stanley Cup without Phil Esposito. Says Bobby Hull: "Boston thought Bobby Orr was going to lead them out of the wilderness. But Orr couldn't do it alone. Orr and Esposito, they complement one another, they make each other better."

Talk to Bobby Orr and he will agree. And he will tell you exactly what Phil Esposito has meant for this team. "He keeps everyone relaxed and loosey," Orr says, a grin on his long face when he talks about the guy the players call Espy. "When he came here he came with a winning spirit that he

Dit Clapper: The "policeman" for the Krauts.

brought from a winning club. He brought us all together and made us believe we could win.

"The minute Espy got there, he changed this whole team. He went around training camp bringing us together. He'd say, 'C'mon guys, I know we can make the playoffs, but we got to stick together.' We did, and we still do. We're like a team of brothers. I know Phil has scored a lot of points, but to my mind he's even more important off the ice. He's the force that holds us together."

On a road trip with the Bruins midway through the 1970–71 season, I saw first-hand how Phil brings the team together. In planes, hotel lobbies or buses, the Bruins seemed to cling physically to the big guy. Four or five Bruins would walk from their hotel to a nearby poolroom, and there was the long-striding Phil leading the way, jokes cracking out of the side of his mouth, laughter roaring in his wake. In a lobby there'd be a knot of Bruins, Phil in the middle, talking, laughing, joking.

On planes he played non-stop euchre games with John (Pie) McKenzie, Johnny (Chief) Bucyk and Fred Stanfield. They play euchre hour after hour, but they know each other so well that rarely, even after four or five hours, does any one of them lose more than a few dollars.

We were flying from Boston to Chicago. As soon as the pilot snapped off the "fasten seat belt" sign, Espy bounded down the aisle to stand next to the seats where Bucyk, Stanfield and McKenzie were seated three-abreast. They flipped down the trays in front of them and the cards were dealt for what might have been the 10,901st hand of euchre this season.

"Hey, Espy, Espy," Wayne (Swoop) Carleton shouted. "How come you are always the one who is standing? Those guys must be winning a lot of money from you."

Espy smiled his sad Mediterranean smile, then shrugged his shoulders, eyes rolling upward. What can I do? he was saying in pantomime, and the other players laughed.

"Espy, Espy," someone else was yelling. Espy turned and faced the front of the plane. He threw out his arms and bellowed, "O, sole mio . . . O mamma mia . . . " Now all the Bruins were laughing.

The goalies do not laugh when they talk about Phil Esposito. "When he gets that puck in front of the net," says Chicago's Gerry Desjardins, "he is all arms and legs and he looks like he's 12-foot wide. He doesn't get excited and rush the shot. He'll make two or three moves with the stick to get you down on the ice and then the game is over. Goal."

In the 1970–71 season Phil Esposito scored more goals over one season, 76, than anyone in the history of the National Hockey League. He easily broke Bobby Hull's record of 58. Sixteen of those goals won games—another record. He collected 76 assists for a total of 152 points—another record that broke his own record of 126 set two years earlier. He collected seven hat tricks, a modern-era record that smashed the old record of four. And for the second time in three years, he was the NHL scoring champion.

He did not do it alone, of course. He was helped beyond measure by the digging in the corners of his wingers, brawny Ken Hodge and the willowy Wayne Cashman. And he was helped on power plays by the accurate passes of Bobby Orr (Phil scored 25 goals on power plays, when the other team was short-handed, and that was another record). The line of Esposito-Hodge-Cashman scored more goals (140) and amassed more points (336) than any line in history.

Let's watch that line in action . . .

The Black Hawks possess the puck at the moment, Pit Martin angling with it across the Bruin blue line. Phil is trailing him, a broad-backed longshoreman among the smaller hockey players, few of whom are as tall as six feet. Phil skates with a long-striding, purposeful nonchalance, his long arms reaching out the stick, trying to poke the puck away from Pit Martin.

Martin whirls, looking to pass the puck. Phil swoops in from Martin's blind side and thrusts the puck toward Bobby Orr, who cuddles it to his stick.

Phil and his wingers wheel in three tight circles, turning now toward the Chicago nets where Phil's kid brother, Tony, crouches, waiting, suddenly tense. The seeming nonchalance is gone from Phil's stride. He comes down the ice building speed: a push off the right foot, a push off the left, then a little leap, streaking toward his brother.

Orr, with the puck, snaps it to Phil at the blue line. Phil flings the puck into the right corner. Ken Hodge bulls his way into the corner, elbowing between two Black Hawks. Esposito is veering toward "the slot," the area 15 or 20 feet in front of the cage, from where the shooter can see an opening into the cage. A Chicago defenseman slams into Phil, trying to move him away, but the defenseman bounces off big Phil as though he had collided with a boulder.

"He is so big and strong," says Bruin coach Tom Johnson. "And he keeps his balance well with that wide stance of his."

In the corner Hodge controls the puck a moment, loses it, gets it back again. He looks for Phil, who is back-skating very slowly away from the cage mouth.

"Espy's long arms, they're what make him so effective around the net," Bobby Orr says. "With that long reach he can stay out maybe 25 feet from the cage. The defensemen can't come out to guard him because they'd leave the rear open. Yet with his long arms Phil can stop a pass 15 or so feet in front of the cage, something most centermen can't do."

Hodge whirls and snaps the puck across the ice, too far out for the goalie to reach. Phil reaches out his long arms and stops the puck. A Black Hawk veers in on him, but Phil turns so his body protects the puck.

"You've seen kids play shinny hockey on a pond," Tom Johnson says, "where one kid tries to keep the puck as long as he can, until

someone takes it away from him. Phil would keep the puck all day."

Phil skates slowly toward the cage. He feints a shot and his brother lunges to the right. Phil sees air between the goalie's left elbow and the side of the cage.

"Phil doesn't have the hardest shot I've ever seen," says Gerry Desjardins. "It's only average speed, but he is very accurate at picking the corners."

Phil slaps the puck toward the opening. The puck skims off the ice on a rising line, zips by Tony's left arm and smashes into the nets, hitting a metal bar with a loud clang, and that clang tells it all: another goal for Phil Esposito.

Phil has been scoring goals against his brother for some 25 years now. It all began when Phil was five and Tony four back in Sault Ste. Marie in Ontario when they played table-hockey games. Phil would draw back a lever and smack a steel ball and Tony would flip a lever to block the shot. "Even then Tony made some tremendous saves," Phil remembers.

A year later they were playing ice hockey. Maybe it was because Phil was the older but Tony was nearly always the goaltender while Phil did the fun thing: He was the shooter.

Some mornings during the winters the boys would arise before dawn. They loaded Tony's pads and other equipment onto a toboggan and pulled it through the dark streets to a rink. There they played Bantam games, happy to get ice-time even at seven in the morning, when the Bantam League games were played.

Phil and Tony played on a neighborhood hockey team. Phil, even then the loud one, was the team's leader. In one game Tony let two long shots skid by him for goals and the team lost, 2—1. Phil skated over to Tony after the game and screamed at him: "You blind jerk, you quit on us." His kid brother began to bawl and Phil turned away, sorry he had said what he didn't mean. He felt even sorrier a few weeks later. His father took Tony to a doctor, who discovered

Tony needed glasses (he now wears contact lenses).

Phil needed all of that competitive drive, though, especially during his teenage years. Around Sault Ste. Marie, where they grow NHL players the way a swamp grows mosquitoes, the hockey buffs said of Phil: "A great stick-handler and a good shooter, but can he skate fast enough for big league hockey? He may be too big and slow."

Phil lost some weight and improved his skating playing junior hockey. After three minor-league years he came up to the Hawks near the end of the 1963–64 season. Immediately he made friends with two kindred souls: superstar Bobby Hull and Chico Maki, and wherever you found Espy, Hull and Maki, you found the laughs.

"Before I met Bobby," Phil says, "I was a bit of a rebel. I'd dropped out of school in the 12th grade. The hell with the world, I thought. I just didn't care all that much about the feelings of other people. I think I've changed. I'll sign autographs now more than I did then. I'll stop to talk to people who come up to say hello. I saw the way Bobby Hull treated people, how nice he could be to people, and that took some of the rough edges off me."

Phil wasn't rough enough for Billy Reay, though. He sent Phil, Ken Hodge and Fred Stanfield to Boston for center Pit Martin, goalie Jack Norris and defenseman Gil Marotte. Pit Martin became a star in Chicago but Norris and Marotte went on to near obscurity. In Boston, meanwhile, Hodge and Esposito became All-Stars and Stanfield centered a line that scored more goals than any line in the league in 1970–71, Esposito's excepted. In the Boston Garden they call the trade the "second Brink's job."

At first Phil was stunned and unhappy about the trade. "Last season Boston was in last place and Chicago was in first place," he told a friend. "Look at all the money I am going to lose in between."

Bobby Hull was just as unhappy. "I lost my right arm,"

he moaned, *"my right arm."*

But coming to the Bruins made Phil Esposito a better hockey player. Feeling the responsibility of being an assistant captain and trying to lift up this losing team, he became a harder-working and more confident player. People around the league noticed. "Phil is getting to be another Jean Beliveau," Punch Imlach, then Toronto's general manager, said one day. "Phil has plenty of confidence now. When he came over from Chicago, he perhaps didn't know whether he could do it or not. Now he knows he can."

In Phil's first season as a Bruin, 1967–68, he led the team in scoring with 21 goals and 40 assists for 61 points. The next year he led the league in scoring with 49 goals and 77 assists for a record-shattering 126 points. And he was named the league's most valuable player. In 1969–70, after finishing second to Bobby Orr in league scoring with 99 points, he led the Bruins in scoring in the Stanley Cup playoffs, setting playoff records for goals with 13 and points with 27.

In 1970–71 he won the scoring championship for the second time in three years. In a close vote, Orr beat him out for the Hart Trophy as the league's Most Valuable Player.

"I'm grateful for the Hart," Orr said at the award ceremony in Montreal. *"But I think it easily could have gone to one of my teammates, Phil Esposito."*

Typically, Phil took his second-place finish in the MVP voting with good nature. "Hey, superstar," he told Orr, "how come I get all the goals and points and you get all the trophies?"

Orr laughed and said, "Because I'm better looking."

"No," Phil said. "I know what the trouble is. I'm jinxed."

Actually Phil *is* superstitious. He wears a lucky turtleneck, carries a medal inside his pads, and has been known to wear the same suit to games when the Bruins were on a winning streak. Various omens hang above his dressing stall.

"I'm not as superstitious as I once was," he told me not

long ago. "Like I don't complain now when Turk and Greenie cross sticks behind me. I was always told that crossed
sticks in the clubhouse means you're going to lose. But now
I ignore them."

He paused. "Still," he said, "I don't like to talk about
injuries. I've never been seriously hurt, a broken wrist once,
that's all, but I think that if you talk about not getting hurt,
that's when you are going to get hurt.

"But I have always been lucky. I am lucky in hockey. You
have to be lucky to score a lot of goals. Some people are lucky
in one thing and not in another. Like they might be lucky
in sports and not in business. But I've also been lucky in
business."

Along with his brother and teammate Fred Stanfield, Phil
owns hockey schools in Weymouth, Mass., and in Sault Ste.
Marie, and he owns a part of a company that makes hockey
equipment.

(Phil has been especially lucky against brother Tony in
Bruin-Black Hawk confrontations. The first time they played
against each other, the game ended in a 2–2 tie, but it was
Phil who scored both Boston goals. In the Stanley Cup
playoffs in 1970, Phil poured five goals past brother Tony as
the Bruins swept the Black Hawks in four straight.)

"The best guy on defense for Chicago is my brother," Phil
says of Tony. "He's the one we have to beat. I think I know
how to do it. Maybe I know where he's a little weak. But I'm
not saying. No, I ain't even going to tell the guys on my own
team how to beat him."

One Esposito who won't watch the two boys play against
each other, even on TV, is their mother. Once Phil scored
twice against his brother. Then, from his home in Salem,
Mass., Phil phoned his mother.

"How could you do that?" Mrs. Esposito shouted at Phil.
"How could you score against your own brother?"

Phil tried to explain. His mother would not listen. When

someone will listen, Phil says: "Tony's my brother, we're close buddies. But not on the ice. I'm out to score against him, and he's out to stop me. That's our business. Sometimes I'll kid him out there, though. When he has made a great save, I'll skate over to him and say, 'You're a lucky so-and-so.' He never answers me."

"Yeah, he talks to me," Tony says. "I ignore him. If I started thinking of him as my brother, it would destroy my concentration."

Tony pauses, and then he says what more and more people in hockey now say of Philip Anthony Esposito: "He'll score against anybody. He's the best centerman there ever was."

The first great Boston centerman was Ralph (Cooney) Weiland, now in hockey's Hall of Fame. In the 1929–30 season Cooney scored 43 goals in 44 games, a rate that was not approached by a modern player until Espy scored 76 in 78 games in 1970–71. Cooney Weiland centered the Bruins' first outstanding line, called The Dynamite Line, and that line helped bring the Stanley Cup to Boston for the first time.

Chapter V

THE CUP TAKES THE MIDNIGHT TRAIN
TO BOSTON

The hockey player strode into the room. He glanced around quickly. The room was empty. He walked to a table and opened a cigar box. He put his hand inside the box.

A look of astonishment—and then anger—spread across the hockey player's face. He picked up the box and stared into it. Empty. He slammed the box onto the table and walked quickly out of the room.

In the hallway he saw the coach of his hockey team, one of the most successful amateur hockey teams in the Boston area during the winter of 1923–24. Amateur hockey teams were drawing as many as 7,000 fans into the old Boston Arena. To keep winning this team was paying its best players, violating amateur rules. After a game the player strolled into a certain room, put his hand inside the cigar box, and took out his money. As the Boston Irish would put it, "Little said is easily meant."

But on this night one star was saying quite a bit. "Where's my money?" he snapped at the coach. "I looked in the cigar box and—"

' We didn't like your attitude out there tonight. We're fining you the money."

"I'll see about that. I'm going to get a lawyer and we'll sue you for the money."

Within days the newspapers were headlining the story of the Great Amateur Hockey Scandal. Sitting in the office of one of the retail stores he owned, the graying Charles F. Adams read the stories in an abstracted way, his mind turning away from the pages toward an idea he had long been considering. At one time Adams had owned the Boston Braves baseball team and the Suffolk Downs Race Track. His primary interest had been in a chain of retail stores, but he understood the risky business of professional sports. He had always thought that Bostonians who liked hockey, like himself, would pay to see pro hockey. Now, he mused, the timing might be just right, the fans in Boston disenchanted enough with the hypocrisy of amateur hockey to come out to see honest-to-God professionals. He decided to apply for a franchise in the seven-year-old National Hockey League.

He got the franchise on November 1,1924, the first ever given to a U.S. team (the Rangers, Chicago, and Detroit were to come into the league two years later). Adams hired Art Ross, a crusty, tough-minded veteran of the hockey wars and then the owner of a Montreal sporting goods store, as his general manager, head coach, scout and one-man front office. Together Adams and Ross began to build a hockey team.

One of their first tasks was to name the team. Adams asked reporters and fans to submit names, but first setting some ground rules. One, since the team's basic colors would be brown with yellow trim (the color combination of Brookside Stores, owned by the promotion -conscious Adams), the name should relate to something brown. Secondly, said Adams, the name should be that of an untamed animal who was big, strong and agile.

Adams scanned hundreds of names and didn't like any of them. One day Art Ross said to him: "My secretary at my Montreal store has a suggestion. How about Bruins? They're big, they're strong and agile."

Adams accepted the name. One suspects, though, that the Bruins might have been named the Bears if a man named Halas in Chicago hadn't baptized a football team the Chicago Bears a few years earlier. Although perhaps a bear might not have been agile enough for Adams' taste.

The aggressive Ross busily signed players in the late fall of 1924, most of them ex-amateurs from around Boston. On Monday, December 1, 1924, in the old Boston Arena, some 7,000 fans applauded as the new Bruins skated onto the ice to play Montreal. In goal was Hec Fowler and the starting five skaters were Jimmy Herberts, Carson Cooper, Herb Mitchell, Bobby Rowe and Fred Harris. Also on that first Bruin team were Bobby Benson, George Carroll, Lloyd Cook, Curley Headley, Stan Jackson, Herb Mitchell, Bernie Morris, George Redding, Werner Schnarr, Normie Shay, Alfie Skinner, Spunk Sparrow, Charles "Doc" Stewart, Red Stuart, and its star and best player, whose No. 3 was retired when he retired in 1933—defenseman Lionel (Hitch) Hitchman.

Montreal beat the Bruins in their debut, 2–1, and losing soon became as familiar to the Bruins as their brown-and-yellow shirts. They won only six games while losing 24 in that season's 30–game schedule. They scored only 49 goals while yielding 119. The team's high scorer, Jimmy Herberts, scored 17, almost one-third of the team's total.

In 1925 Adams and Ross looked at a slew of hockey players, running them in and out of Boston in boxcar lots, swapping with other teams in frenetic search for a straw of gold in a haystack. "We have so many players coming in and

out of here," Charles Adams once told a friend, "that I
sometimes think we have three hockey teams—one coming,
one going, and one playing."

But it helped. The Bruins rose from last to fourth (in a
seven-team league) in 1925–26, their second season, with a
17–15–4 record. During the off-season Adams learned that
two of the Patrick brothers, Les and Frank, wanted to sell the
stars of their Pacific Coast League for some needed cash.
Adams decided that here was a way to equalize the talent in
the NHL, lifting the new U.S. teams to the level of the old-
line Canadian teams. He bought all the stars of the Pacific
Coast League. He picked three of the best for his Bruins and
re-sold the others to the newly franchised U.S. teams, the
Rangers, Black Hawks and Detroit Cougars.

Adams kept Harry Oliver, a shifty, high-scoring forward.
And he kept Perk Galbraith, another quick-skating winger.
The third player he kept was the one he and Ross had bought
the league to get: a balding 24-year-old defenseman named
Eddie Shore.

Some six years earlier Eddie Shore never had played a
serious game of hockey. Though he had grown up in western
Canada, he had helped till a farm for his father as a boy, and
he had always been more interested in baseball than hockey.
He and his brother Aubrey went off to college together. One
wintry day they were discussing the school's hockey team.
Eddie allowed as how he might just try out for the hockey
team.

"Hah," said Aubrey. "You'd never make a hockey player.
You're not strong enough, you're not quick enough."

A hot competitive flame had always burned inside Eddie.
He could do anything—stack hay, cut grass, hit a ball—and
do it better than most anyone. Now that flame flared.

"Who says I can't?" he snapped at his brother. "Anybody
could be a hockey player."

For the next few weeks, although the temperature hovered

at some 30 degrees below zero, Eddie skated and stick handled on the school's outdoor rink, teaching himself to be a hockey player. He made the college team. A year later he made a pro team, the Edmonton Flyers, and soon they were calling Eddie Shore the Edmonton Express, the wild defenseman who barged down the ice, bowling over people, in a pell-mell dash for the nets. People jammed arenas to see him play, eyes fixed on him when he took the puck. They stood and screamed as he sped off on one of those wild dashes for a score. You never knew when this bull might break loose, and he gave the game—and the Bruins—a new home run kind of excitement.

With Shore, Harry Oliver and Frank Frederickson the stars, the Bruins finished second in the NHL's American Division in 1926—27. In the playoffs the Bruins beat Chicago and the Rangers and rose to the final round, suddenly within a best-of-three-game series of being the first U.S. team to win the Stanley Cup.

It was not to be. The Ottawa Senators beat the Bruins twice, with two other games ending in ties, to win the cup. But the following season, 1927–28, Charles Adams got one small measure of revenge: The New York Rangers, employing the stars that Adams had shuttled to New York from the old Pacific Coast League, became the first U.S. team to win the Cup. The Bruins had finished first in the American Division of the two-division league, but bowed to the Rangers in the opening round.

By now Boston was being called "hockey-mad" by visiting writers from New York and Chicago. Each hockey night the small Boston Arena was filled, spectators standing and sitting in the aisles. In New York the shrewd Tex Rickard had finished building Madison Square Garden and he started dreaming of a chain of indoor sports arenas across the country. His Madison Square Garden Corporation decided to build the Boston Garden, with a capacity of over 15,000, and

Frankie Brimsek: "Mr. Zero" bats away another puck.

by the start of the 1928–29 NHL season the new Boston
Garden stood erect and hulking, abutting the North Station
on Causeway Street.

On November 20, 1928, the Bruins played their first game
in the Garden. Among the thousands who lined up on
Causeway Street waiting to enter was a young, unemployed
accountant, Edward J. Powers.

"We knew this was going to be an exciting team and
everyone wanted to see the first game in the Garden," says
Powers, who is now the president of the Garden. "The Bruins
had what we called The Dynamite Line. There was Cooney
Weiland at center, Dit Clapper and Dutch Gainor on the
wings. The defensemen were Eddie Shore and Hitch Hitchman, and the goalie was a young kid everyone had high
hopes for—Tiny Thompson. And there was a real fine second
line with Doc Carson at center, and Harry Oliver and Perk
Galbraith on the wings.

"Everyone in Boston wanted a ticket to see the game.
People were saying it was easier to buy a seat on the Stock
Exchange than to get a ticket to this game. Anyway, when
they opened the doors everyone started to push. The doors
gave way, and people just ran over the flattened doors and
into the Garden."

The attendance was estimated at 17,000, and that is still
the unofficial high for a hockey game in the Garden, or
"the gah-den," as most of the people in that crowd called it.
They howled insults at the officials and screamed encourage-
ment to their Bruins, and they left muttering at their shoe-
tops, the Bruins 1–0 losers.

They came back for the next game screaming just as loudly. For a startling phenomenon was taking place. The first
Big Bad Bruin, Eddie Shore, with his bold charges that
bloodied both himself and opponents, was giving the Bruins
the hit-'em-in-the-mouth character that would become the
hallmark of this team. And those exciting charges were

bringing to the Garden the kind of fan who liked his hockey
to be as physical as a clenched fist. Eddie Shore was shaping
the character of a team and the character of its fans. Once the
late poet, Robert Frost, counseled President John F. Ken-
nedy to be "more Irish and less Boston"—that is, more
pugnacious and less gentlemanly. Eddie Shore was making
the Bruins more Irish and less Boston.

The canny Art Ross devised stunts to build up Shore as
an even greater drawing card—much to Shore's own dismay.
Before a game the band would strike up *Hail to the Chief.* Out
on the rink skated Shore, wearing a long matador's cape. A
valet followed him, helped the pink-faced Shore to remove
the cape, and the great one—applauded by his loyal subjects
—was ready to play.

Once, after this royal introduction, the New York Americans suddenly rolled a red carpet onto the ice—and out
jumped one of their smaller players, Rabbit McVeigh. He
blew a kiss at Shore, who heatedly swore at the Rabbit.
Later Shore swore at Ross, insisting he would never wear the
cape again, and after a while Ross saw he couldn't raise
Shore any higher in the affections of the Bruin fans. He retired the cape to a dusty closet.

Shore was as well liked by most of the Bruins. They talked
in awe of his physical toughness. Once, in a scrimmage, a
swinging blade knifed into Shore's ear. The team doctor
insisted he would have to amputate the ear. But Shore, who
prided himself on his medical knowledge (all self-taught),
insisted on another opinion. The next doctor said: amputate.
You're wrong, Shore said, going to another doctor. Finally he
found one doctor who said he could sew the ear together.
And he did, directed by Shore, who refused ether and calmly
showed the doctor where to sew. Forty years later, when
many of those doctors were dead, Eddie Shore still had his
ear.

He was incredibly helpful to young players whom he

thought talented. Midway through the 1928–29 season the Bruins signed George Owen, a defenseman who had been a popular star at Harvard. He was paid some $12,000, an incredible sum in those days. Owen immediately made the investment pay off by bringing into Bruin games those proper Bostonians who had long thought of professional hockey— and professional football and baseball, too—as something smelly.

"Here I was coming into the team with all that publicity and bonus money," Owen says, now a stocks and bonds man in Boston. "Shore could have said, 'OK, kid, let me see what you can do with your big reputation.' Instead he covered for me during my first few games. He often said, 'Everybody on this team should be working for the other fellow as well as for himself. We are all pulling together to win.' "

The other star of that 1928–29 team was winger Dit Clapper, a raw-boned hulking skater built much like today's Phil Esposito. Clapper stood 6–1, weighed 195, "a tremendous physical specimen, even among the players, who were all built well themselves," George Owen says. "At that time the Canadian heavyweight champion was Lionel Conacher, who also played hockey. We always felt that Dit could have beat Conacher in a boxing ring."

During a Boston-Ottawa brawl one night, an Ottawa player charged into Clapper, fists flying. Dit knocked him sprawling with one righthanded chop to the jaw. Another player swung at him. Clapper ducked, lashed out that right hand, and down dropped the second player, legs splayed. A third took a run at him. Clapper hooked the right into his jaw and down went the third.

"Three punches, three men down," Owen says. "And not one of those punches traveled more than six inches. And, remember, he was throwing them while standing on skates. He could have been a great fighter except that I don't think he was mean enough. I don't think Dit Clapper ever did a nasty thing in his life."

Clapper and Eddie Shore are now in Hockey's Hall of Fame. In fact, of the 17 players on that 1928–29 team, seven are now in the Hall of Fame along with their coach, Art Ross. They are: Shore, Clapper, goalie Tiny Thompson, and fowards Frank Fredrickson, Mickey MacKay, Ralph (Cooney) Weiland, and the shifty center and high scorer of the team, Harry Oliver.

They played a more patterned game than the hockey of today, George Owen says. "The blue line was the focus of the operation. It was there that the play developed. With a lot of passing, you tried to get the puck to someone open and penetrate. There was always a sense of excitement: at any moment someone could burst free. There was little of this business that you have today where they throw the puck back of the cage and go in after it.

"There was not as much fore-checking as there is today. You usually let the other team come up almost to the blue line before you did much checking. You didn't want to risk someone breaking open behind you. There was more face-to-face checking than today, where they ram people from behind. I would not say that the game was rougher than it is today—it is about as rough now as it was then—but there was one thing you could do that the players today can't do. Those glass partitions didn't run all the way around the rink, so with a good body check you could hip the other guy up into the stands."

Brawling, hipping and scoring, the Bruins won 26 games, lost 13 and tied 5 to finish first in the American Division for the second-straight year. For the third-straight year they were in the playoffs.

They met the Canadiens and eliminated them in three straight games. Now they took on the Rangers in the first Stanley Cup final between two U.S. teams.

The best-of-three series opened in Boston, and fans assem-

bled in block-long lines to buy tickets. They talked respect-
fully of the Ranger defense, which had allowed only one goal
so far in four Stanley Cup games. But in Boston the Bruins
were 8–5 favorites to win.

The Rangers had Johnny Roach at goal and Ching Johnson and Taffie Abel on defense. The first-line center was
Frank Boucher, with Bun and Bill Cook on the wings. One of
the second-line Ranger forwards was Paul Thompson, the
brother of Bruin goalie Tiny Thompson, a matchup in Stanley Cup play that two Esposito brothers, then unborn, would
duplicate some 40 years later.

The Bruins scored first. Dit Clapper burst through the
Ranger defense and slammed the puck at Roach. The rubber
ricocheted off the goalie's pads and flew directly back to
Clapper as he careened toward the net. Although startled to
see the puck again so soon, the burly Dit slapped another
shot at the cage, and this one flew by the helpless Roach into
the nets.

The huge standing-room-only crowd, estimated at 18,000
by some of the New York writers, stood, roared, screamed,
blew trumpets and cascaded a snowstorm of paper onto the
ice. When the ice was cleared, the Rangers counterattacked,
jerked out of their defensive mood by that goal. Paul Thompson popped a shot at his brother, Tiny kicking the puck away
at the last micro-second. His brother shot again, and again
Tiny batted away the puck.

Suddenly, there was Boston's Dutch Gainor with the puck,
streaking in his shifty-hipped way down the ice. He angled
toward the cage, slamming the puck at Roach, who dived
and missed it, the black rubber snapping the nets. *Goal!* The
Bruins led, 2–0, and again the Garden roof seemed to lift with
the roaring, another blizzard of white paper floating down on
the ice.

The ice was cleared, play resumed. A minute later Art
Ross sent out a new line, replacing Gainor, and again there

was roaring and screaming and the blaring of trumpets as the happy Boston fans saluted Gainor.

The Bruins won the game, 2–0. That night both teams boarded the midnight train to New York for the second game the next night, Good Friday, in New York at Madison Square Garden. New York had to win to stay alive.

Late in the first period Harry Oliver collected the puck at center-ice, swept by Taffie Abel and Sparky Vail, and unleashed a close-in shot that Roach could not stop. The Bruins led, 1–0, a goal that was greeted by a thin chorus of cheers from the small knot of Bruins rooters who had come down from Boston for the game.

The Bruins nurtured that 1–0 lead into the third period, the Ranger fans silent now, some 15,000 in the packed Garden, hushed in the expectancy of defeat. They saw the Rangers' Butch Keeling take the puck at the blue line and suddenly, unexpectedly, fire it at the Boston net. Caught by surprise, Tiny Thompson turned too late to watch the puck fly by his right elbow and crash into the top of the cage.

The Ranger fans came to their feet, their time to roar, and they roared for five minutes, on and on and on, so loud that play could not resume, New York's turn now to layer the ice with swirling white paper.

Finally the game started again. Anxiously the Ranger fans eyed the clock, hoping the game would go into overtime where the Rangers would have a chance to score early and hold off the Bruins on this small rink. Now there were only two minutes remaining. The clever Harry Oliver took the puck across the blue line and saw teammate Bill Carson skating to his right and trailing slightly behind him. Oliver veered toward the boards, skated around Taffie Abel, drawing the Ranger defense toward them. Then he shot a pass across ice to Carson, who was skating toward the open side of the Ranger cage. Carson took the pass and shot in one blurred motion, the puck zipping by goalie Roach's left hip and

The Krauts: Schmidt (15) swoops in to slap puck by fallen Ranger goalie Bert Gardiner.

socking into the cage.

"A goal, a goal," the tiny band of Bruin rooters was shouting. It was the goal that won the first Stanley Cup for the Boston Bruins, the gong sounding minutes later, the Bruins 2–1 winners and Stanley Cup champions. On the ice the Bruins hugged and screamed and pounded each other on the backs. They shook the hands of each Ranger. Then they skated off the ice, player-coach Cy Denneny carrying the Stanley Cup. That night the Cup was carried onto the midnight train out of Penn Station, the happy Bruin players putting it in the upper berth of a Pullman, taking the Stanley Cup north and home to Boston.

Chapter VI

EDDIE SHORE
THE EDMONTON EXPRESS

You are sitting with the old-timers in the NHL press boxes or in the hotel lobbies around the league. They are telling, with much laughter, some of the amazing Eddie Shore stories.

He fancied himself as a doctor who had his own prescription for a cold—12 drops of iodine taken *internally*. Once he prescribed the iodine for a goalie, Ken Schinkel. Later Schinkel said to a friend: "I'll tell you something—it worked."

Shore claimed to be just as knowing about curing farm animals, for after all he had attended an agricultural college for a short while. Once Shore and a few friends were driving through upstate New York. They stopped at a farm-house for directions. After getting the directions and strolling back to the car, Shore mentioned to the farmer that he'd cared for some 200 head of cattle back on his father's farm in Saskatchewan. The farmer asked Shore if he had ever heard of a certain illness among cows.

"Sure," Eddie said. "You have that trouble here?"

"Yep," said the farmer. "See that cow over there? She's ailing with it."

"Bring the cow here," Eddie commanded.

The farmer trotted the cow over to Eddie. The brawny 5–10, 190-pound Shore rolled up his shirt sleeve and forced open the cow's jaws. He stuck his fist down the cow's throat, ramming it up and down several times while the cow stomped and mooed, kicking up dust.

Shore jerked out his arm, now gooey to the elbow after its trip down the cow's gullet. Without bothering to towel off the goo, Eddie rolled down his shirt sleeve. "We fixed that problem many times back on the farm," he told the astonished farmer and his friends. He watched the cow galloping frantically to the safety of the barn. "She'll be as good as new," he said.

Eddie Shore was just as confident on the ice. He became famous as The Edmonton Express because of his rink-length dashes toward goal, knocking down anyone who got in his way. Or, as often as not, it was Shore who was knocked down. "The thing about Eddie," says a contemporary, George Owen, "was that when he streaked down the ice with those long strides of his and crashed into people, he was as likely to hurt himself as he was to hurt other people. But that never stopped him. He kept right on coming."

In Eddie's 19 years of professional hockey, doctors sewed 978 stitches into his bony face and concrete-hard body. His back was fractured, his hip broken, a collarbone snapped. His nose was broken 14 times, Both eyeballs were slashed by skates. Nearly every one of his teeth had been knocked out of his mouth.

Once, in a 1929 game, the entire Montreal team decided to savage him. For two and a half periods the Montreal players swung at him with their sticks, and near the end of the game blood was streaming down Eddie's face, gushing out of a deep cut across his left eye.

Eddie wiped away the blood and kept on playing, strips of tape plastered across his wounds. In the final minute the brawny Babe Siebert smashed into Eddie, cracking his stick across Eddie's face.

Eddie collapsed onto the ice, teeth spilling out of his mouth. For 14 minutes he did not move while a trainer tried to bring him back to consciousness. He was still unconscious when his teammates carted him off the ice, the blood driping off his face, leaving a red-on-white trail. At a hospital doctors revived Eddie and found that the Montreal players had done their work well. They had broken Eddie's nose, smashed three of his teeth, blackened both eyes, torn open a gash across his cheekbone and sliced a two-inch wound above his eye.

Eddie came back to play the Bruins' next game. Inside him there flamed the desire to be the best at whatever he did, refusing to be stopped or pushed aside by pain. He had been that way since he was a boy on his father's farm. Once, when he was nine, he tried to break in a Shetland pony. A friend was watching from outside the corral. As Eddie mounted the pony, it bucked, ramming its head into Eddie's nose, breaking the nose.

A wave of nausea swept over young Eddie, his vision blurring, the corral whirling dizzingly around him. The salty taste of blood seeped into his mouth. He heard his friend yelling, "Stick it out, Eddie, stick it out."

Eddie Shore stuck it out, breaking that pony and dozens of other bucking horses on his father's farm. He played hockey as though he were riding a bucking bronc, trying to dominate his opponents with the sheer power of his charges up the ice.

"Shore would roar up the ice like a human catapult," Ed Fitzgerald once wrote in Sport Magazine "leading the two fastest forwards on the team. Zooming toward the goal he would unleash a bullet-like drive—but *not* at the net. Instead, he would rifle the puck against the backboards and, head lowered like a vengeful bull, smash his way through the enemy defense as though it were so much paper. Eddie was so fast that he could retrieve the puck as it came off the boards, pass it back to his forwards, and more often than not grin sardonically as his teammates angled it home for a goal."

Those sardonic grins did not make him any favorite among opposing players. And his bitter debates with Art Ross over money and other matters never made him a favorite with the Bruins' front office. He was often suspended or fined by the NHL for fighting. When the charter members of the Hockey Hall of Fame were elected in the 1940s, Eddie Shore was not among those voted into the shrine. Among those who had picked the first Hall of Famers was Art Ross. Newspapermen wrote columns ridiculing this snub of Eddie Shore. In his time he had been called "the Babe Ruth of Hockey." As hockey's first superstar, he had pulled the NHL through the bleak depression years of the thirties, drawing huge crowds wherever the Bruins played. The committee voted again and Eddie Shore entered the Hall of Fame.

Now, the bitterness fading with the years, the old-timers recall the fortitude of the man more than his meanness. Once he rammed into the goal post during a game at the old Madison Square Garden. He limped off the ice, bent over, with three broken ribs. A doctor took him to a hotel room. In his book, *Bobby Orr and the Big Bad Bruins*, Stan Fischler tells what happened:

"Now Eddie," the doctor cautioned, "I want you to stay in your room until I can come back and take you over to the hospital."

The doctor, who should have known better, assumed that Shore's lack of response indicated compliance. He left the hotel, signed up for a hospital room and returned to Shore's room to escort the wounded player to the infirmary. But he found the door wide open and no trace of the player and his baggage. Eddie had stumbled to the lobby and had hailed a cab to Grand Central Station, where he had purchased a ticket for the late train to Montreal. He arrived in time for the game with the Canadiens and scored two goals and an assist.

Once, on his way to catch a train to Boston, Shore was stuck in traffic. He missed the train. He borrowed a friend's car and started driving into the fury of a January blizzard toward Montreal. The car careened off the road and skidded into a ditch. Shore borrowed a farmer's horse and hauled out the car. The windshield wipers froze to a stop. Shore ripped out the windshield and drove straight on, the freezing wind and snow whipping into his face.

He drove into Montreal with one hand frozen onto the wheel. Art Ross took one look at Eddie's bluish face and hands and told him to go to his room and rest. "You're in no shape to play tonight," Ross told Eddie.

But Eddie Shore had not driven 24 hours through a blizzard to sit out a game in a hotel room. That night he played nearly the entire game, for players were not shifted on and off the ice as often as today. And that night Eddie Shore scored the winning goal.

Eddie Shore astonished his fellow hockey players for one other reason: He had started playing the game rather late in life—when he was almost 20. Most Canadian kids are playing shinney hockey as soon as they can walk. Eddie was born in Fort Qu'Appelle, Saskatchewan, in western Canada in 1902. When he was two, his father and mother moved to Cupar, another town in Saskatchewan, to settle on a rolling farm of some 36 square miles. "We had about 400 head of horses and 600 herd of cattle," Eddie once told SPORT's

Ed Fitzgerald. Young Eddie liked to break in horses and all those hours on bucking ponies, Eddie believes, built up the body and legs that made him such a dynamo on ice.

His favorite sports were baseball and soccer. "There were quite a number of Americans farming in the area," Eddie says, "and we played a lot of baseball." Eddie's brother, Aubrey, was a good hockey player but Eddie played only one game during all his high school years. He had driven a local team to another town for a game, and when someone got sick and couldn't play, Eddie filled in. But the game did not excite him; he preferred baseball.

Then Aubrey challenged him to be a hockey player while they both were attending agricultural college. Soon Eddie was among the best in the school.

His father lost his farm after some bad investments. Eddie dropped out of college and decided on a career in this game he had only recently learned. With those wild dashes up and down the ice and a willingness to mix it at the drop of a glove, he soon became the terror of an amateur hockey league and then the professional Pacific Coast League. Bought by Charles Adams in 1926 along with other stars of the Pacific Coast league, Eddie was an immediate sensation in Boston at the start of the '26–27 season. In the Boston *Transcript* a reporter described Shore's first game as a Bruin on November 16, 1926: "Eddie Shore caught the fancy of the fans. The new defenseman is tall, yet sturdily built. His speed is exceptional and he handles his body and stick well."

Those were the first of millions of words to be written by NHL writers about Eddie Shore. Sports columnist John Lardner once wrote: "He is the only man in hockey generally known to the people who ignore hockey."

Those wild charges down the ice put him in the penalty box more minutes than any other Bruin that 1926–27 season, a distinction he would maintain during his first seven seasons in the league. In 1927–28 he led the team in assists as the

The Bruins of the 1930s were the Bruins of Eddie Shore. Four times in the decade Shore won the Hart Trophy as Most Valuable Player.

Bruins finished first in the American Division. The next year, after finishing first again, the team won the Stanley Cup. The Bruins were first again in the American Division the next two seasons, 1929–30 and 1930–31, but bowed in the playoffs both years to the team that would be a Boston nemesis even unto 1971: the Montreal Canadiens.

During Eddie Shore's next eight years with the Bruins, the team finished first four times and second two times. In those years the team's high scorers were people like Cooney Weiland, later a coach at Harvard, who banged home an astonishing 43 goals in 44 games in 1929–30, a rate that was not approached by any NHL player until 1970–71 when another Bruin, Phil Esposito, knocked in 76 goals in 78 games. In the 1930s the high scorers were Marty Barry and Bill Cowley, with big Dit Clapper always high in goals and assists, along with The Kraut Line of Milt Schmidt, Bobby Bauer and Woody Dumart. In the goal was the huge, easy-going Cecil "Tiny" Thompson, now among the great ones in hockey's Hall of Fame. But always, in the minds of those who played against the Bruins and those who watched them, there was Eddie Shore.

Four times during the Thirties—1932–33, 1934–35, 1935–36, 1937–38—Eddie Shore won the Dr. David A. Hart Trophy as the league's Most Valuable Player. He was always in the headlines: "Shore Fined $100 for Fighting." "Shore Called Too Brutal for Hockey." "Coach Demands Shore's Ouster for Violent Conduct."

The Get Rid of Shore chorus reached a crescendo late in 1933 when Shore hit Toronto's Ace Bailey from the rear, flipping Ace onto the ice. Ace's head struck the ice with a dull thud. His legs twitched convulsively as a trainer and players rushed to him. They carried him off the ice and rushed him to a hospital. Surgeons knifed into the skull to repair damaged tissue, then tapped his spine to drain off fluid. For two weeks Ace Bailey's life was suspended on a thread; each hospital bulletin listed his condition as critical.

The NHL's managing director, Frank Patrick, suspended Shore. Connie Smythe, the Maple Leaf coach, said that the Leafs never again would play the Bruins with Shore in the lineup. The league began an investigation of the incident. While the investigation was going on, Ace Bailey began to improve. After the investigation the NHL absolved Eddie Shore of any deliberate intent to injure Bailey. And when the Ace recovered fully, though he never could play another game of hockey, he agreed there had been no maliciousness by Shore. "That's the style of hockey game Shore plays," he said. "I was just unlucky enough to be on the receiving end."

Eddie was popular with his own teammates. But they were careful never to tell him about any physical ailment that was bothering them. Eddie considered himself as expert on human ills as he was in diagnosing the ills of animals. He boasted that twice he had cured himself of cancer.

Once a teammate idly mentioned to Eddie that he'd been bothered by an aching shoulder. Eddie examined the shoulder." "Nothing serious," he said in his best bed-side fashion. "I'll fix it in a minute."

Eddie grabbed the shoulder. "No, Eddie, no," begged the player, as Eddie began to pull at the shoulder so violently it seemed he might wrench the arm from its socket. But Eddie held on, jerking and tugging for some five minutes.

He stopped, breathing heavily. "Feels all right now, doesn't it?" he asked.

The player gripped the sore shoulder. "I can't tell," he said. "It's numb."

Once a Bruin told another: "Don't ever tell Eddie you haven't had your appendix out. He might try to operate right on the clubhouse floor."

In his years with the Bruins Eddie earned top dollar. At the time there was a ceiling on NHL salaries, but Eddie, it was suspected, got two to three times the limit. He saved the money and in 1939 bought something he had always wanted: a hockey team. He got the minor league Springfield Indians for $16,000 cash and a note for $26,000 more. At first Ross did not want to let hockey's top crowd-pleaser leave Boston, although the 37-year-old Shore now was well past his prime. After bitter squabbling, Ross traded Eddie to the New York Americans, who permitted him to play for Springfield as long as he shuttled to New York to fill Madison Square Garden for American home games. He finished the 1939–40 season with the Americans, helping them into the playoffs. In the playoffs he said goodbye to big league hockey with two assists. He went back to Springfield where he trained dozens of young players for the NHL.

He could be as tough with young players as he himself had been with opponents. He growled at his goalies for flopping onto the ice to block shots, leaving themselves wide open for the high shot. When a goalie was unlucky enough to be caught flopping onto the ice during practice, Shore tied one of the goalie's wrists to the top of the cage. Then Shore would scream, "Now let's see you fall on the ice, you numbskull."

The Eddie Shore years, for the Bruins, were winning years. But from 1929 through 1938, the Bruins could not win the big prize: the Stanley Cup. In 1929–30 they reached the final round where they bowed, three games to two, to Howie Morenz and Les Canadiens. From 1930 to 1938 they did not get past the opening round of the seven playoffs they entered. By the start of the 1938–39 season, however, Art Ross had built a team that many still consider the best of all time. On defense it had the veterans Eddie Shore and Dit Clapper, plus a young goalie everyone called Mr. Zero for his many shutouts. There was a sub on that team who would win fame and a nickname at the end of the 1938—39 season: Mel Hill. But there were three players on the 1938—39 Bruins who gave that team its identity in hockey history, three guys everyone called the Krauts.

Chapter VII

THE KRAUTS
MILT, BOBBY AND WOODY

"You have got to give him a chance, Mr. Ross," Woody said.

"He's really a great player," Bobby said. "He's younger than we are, but we've seen him play back in Kitchener, and he can skate faster and shoot harder than either one of us."

Art Ross rubbed a long finger across his chin, reflecting on what these two young hockey players, Bobby Bauer and Woody Dumart, were telling him. Bauer and Dumart had come out of Kitchener in Ontario, an area of German-Canadians. The slight 5–foot–6, 160-pound Bauer skated with a shifty speed and the knack of anticipating what was going to happen, passing the puck to the open man. The burly 190-pound Dumart hit opposing wingers with a savage fierceness that shook the boards, excelled on defense, and shot harder than anyone on the Bruins.

"These boys are going to be real good hockey players in a year or so," Ross had told Dit Clapper and Eddie Shore.

And, he thought, if this boy back in Kitchener is half as good as Bauer and Dumart think he is, he must be one whiz-bang of a hockey player.

"What's this young fellow's name again?" Art Ross asked Dumart and Bauer.

"His name is Milt Schmidt, Mr. Ross."

"I'll write him a letter and invite him to our tryout camp at Hershey next fall."

Art Ross wrote to Milt Schmidt and got this reply:

"Dear Mr. Ross: Thank you for the invitation. I will be there. I am looking for a job now to pay my way from Kitchener to Hershey. Thank you, Milt Schmidt."

At the camp at Hershey in the fall of 1936, Art Ross blinked when he saw the speed and hard shooting of Schmidt. He liked the way the three boys from Kitchener played together on the same line, Schmidt at center with Bauer on the rightwing and Dumart on the leftwing. Ross sent the trio to Providence to get experience. Because of their German ancestry, they were soon nicknamed The Kraut Line.

"The first time the Krauts were together as a line was in Providence in that 1936 season," Schmidt says. "We didn't have much experience, of course, but we worked well together because each of us had something to offer the others. Bobby Bauer was the smallest, and he was the brains of the line. Off the ice Bobby was always reading or studying something, and he was a good hockey student. Woody Dumart was the best defensive player of the Krauts. And being the biggest—he was as big as anyone on the team—he could battle around that cage, and he had a great hard shot. Off the ice he was a very quiet person who minded his own business."

Milt Schmidt doesn't like to talk about himself as a hockey player but he doesn't have to. A sharp-featured man with graying hair who likes narrow-lapeled two-button suits, Milt Schmidt can let his record speak for himself. At the start of the 1971–72 season he ranked as the Bruins' all-time second-leading scorer, trailing only Johnny Bucyk. In his career he scored 229 goals and 346 assists for 575 points. He led the league in scoring in 1940. In 1951 he won the Hart Trophy as the league's Most Valuable Player. Today the general manager of the Bruins is one of the 16 Bruins in Hockey's Hall of Fame.

Bobby Bauer, who died in the mid-1960s, was never a Big Bad Bruin. Only three Bruins in history have won the Lady Byng Trophy awarded each year for gentlemanly conduct. One was Don McKenney, who won it once. Johnny Bucyk, 1970–71, is another. And Bobby Bauer won it three times— in 1939–40, 1940–41 and 1946–47. Though not considered the high scorer that Schmidt and Dumart were, he scored 30 goals in 1946–47, the most goals scored in one season by any of the Krauts.

Woody Dumart ranks sixth among all Boston scorers. He collected 211 goals and 218 assists for a total of 429 points. He is now the owner of a Boston sporting goods store and the official scorer at Garden hockey games.

A look at the scoring statistics of the Krauts shows you how evenly matched they were as hockey players and how they obviously helped each other to score. Here are their scoring records as a line from 1936 to 1947, when Bauer retired.

	Gls.	Assts.	Pts.	Playoff Gls.	Assts.	Pts.
Bobby Bauer rw	123	137	260	10	9	19
Milt Schmidt c	120	171	291	14	14	28
Woody Dumart lw	131	125	256	8	10	18
	—	—	—	—	—	—
	374	433	807	32	33	65

As close as the Krauts were on the ice in their scoring records, they were even closer off the ice. Like the Three Musketeers, they traveled together, they lived near each other at home, they relaxed together. They even enlisted in the Royal Canadian Air Force together at the start of World War II. They always negotiated their contracts together,

walking shoulder to shoulder into Art Ross' office and asking
for exactly the same amount of money.

A SPORT Magazine writer, Lee Greene, once asked
Schmidt why he didn't ask more money for himself, since he
was generally considered to be the star of the Krauts. "We
had grown up together," Schmidt replied, "we were lifetime
friends, and we always felt that if each of us got exactly the
same as the others, there would never be any jealousy or
discontent among us.

"It generally worked well, although in the 1940 season
we were all holdouts because Mr. Ross turned us down for a
$500 raise—and after we'd finished one-two-three in the
league scoring."

It did work well in the long run "After we ended our
careers," Schmidt said, "Bobby in 1947, Woody in 1951 and
me in 1954, we were just as good friends as when we started
out."

On the walls of the office of Milt Schmidt, the Bruins' general manager, are framed oil portraits of the Krauts—Milt
Schmidt, No. 15, Bobby Bauer, No. 17, and Woody Dumart,
No. 14. Looking up at those portraits, Milt recalls the great
moments of the Kraut Line:

"The biggest thrill of my career came in 1942. It was our
last game in the Garden. The next day we flew to Canada
together to enlist in the RCAF. We beat the Canadiens that
night something like 8–1 and the Krauts got something like
eight or nine points. When the game was over the players of
both teams picked us up and skated us off the ice while the
organist played 'Auld Lang Syne.' I'll never forget it. Next
to that was the night we came back from the war to the
Bruins in 1945. The ovation they gave the Krauts when we
came back onto the ice, it made me cry."

There were thousands who cried in the Boston Garden on a
night in 1952. As part of a Milt Schmidt-Woody Dumart
Night, the Bruins coaxed Bobby Bauer out of retirement to

"I've seen courageous guys in this game," Art Ross once said, "but this Ezinicki beats them all." Wild Bill was a tough battler.

play one more game—one last stand for the Kraut Line.

At the time Milt Schmidt had scored 199 goals. There were a lot of sentimental well-wishers in the Garden that night who hoped they would see the Kraut Line together when Schmidt scored that 200th goal. But even the most sentimental forgot that hope when they saw the pudgy Bobby Bauer wobble onto the ice before the game, looking as though he hadn't skated in years.

Before the game fans and players bestowed gifts on the Krauts. As the Krauts skated off, together of course, every person in the Garden stood and applauded—including the Bruins' opponents that night, the Chicago Black Hawks.

But when the game began the Hawks became all business, checking Bruins into the boards. Soon after, coach Lynn Patrick turned toward where numbers 15, 17 and 14 were sitting on the bench and said, "Ok, Krauts, get in there."

The Krauts stood up and started to climb over the boards, sticks in hands. The packed crowd in the Garden began to roar as Schmidt, Dumart and Bauer—for this one last game—skated onto the ice. Though still rocking on his skates, Bobby Bauer retrieved the puck near the blue line, neatly dodged a check by a Hawk and passed the puck to Woody Dumart at center-ice. Woody dashed for the net and slammed the puck on a low line at goalie Harry Lumley.

Lumley kicked out a leg, the puck bouncing off his pads. Milt Schmidt swooped in front of the net, cozied the puck to his stick and whisked it by Lumley.

Goal No. 200 for Milt Schmidt. Woody Dumart dived into the cage, retrieved the puck and handed it to Schmidt. With the crowd's roar raining down on him, a white-faced Milt stood at center-ice, the other two Krauts skating around him in small circles, whacking him on the back with their sticks. Then, in the suddenly hushed Garden, announcer Frank Fallon's voice boomed: "Boston goal by Schmidt, with assists from Dumart and Bauer!"

The Garden filled with a happy roar, this one last hurrah for the Krauts. And for many fans, this last sweet hurrah brought back a flood of memories, memories of two Stanley Cups won by what may have been the greatest hockey team ever.

Chapter VIII

THE 1938–41 BRUINS
BOSTON'S FIRST GREAT SCORING MACHINE

"It took a war to break up that team," the old-timer was saying one day in Boston Garden. "Nothing on ice could have done it from that day to this."

"They were," said Art Ross, "the best team I ever saw in my life."

Fans in New York might argue that the Rangers of 1941–42, with Bryan Hextall, Phil Watson and Lynn Patrick, were every bit as good as that Bruin team of 1938 to 1941. Fans in Detroit, Chicago and Montreal might nominate teams of the 1950s and 1960s as the best ever. But consider some of these debating points for that Bruin team of the Krauts, Frankie Brimsek, Eddie Shore, Bill Cowley, Roy Conacher and Mel (Sudden Death) Hill:

It finished first three straight seasons and won the Stanley Cup two of those years. One year it lost only eight games of 48.

In 1939–40 four Bruins were the league's top four scorers: Milt Schmidt finished first with 52 points and was trailed by the other two Krauts, Bobby Bauer and Woody Dumart, each with 43, and centerman Bill Cowley with 40.

The team's defense was at least as formidable as its offense. During one stretch of seven games in 1938–39, Frankie (Mr. Zero) Brimsek registered six shutouts. That season, and again in 1941–42, he was voted the league's outstanding goalie.

"In fact," Art Ross once told SPORT's Lee Greene, "our defense used to do something that would be suicidal today. I used to order my forwards to play outside when back-checking against the opposing wings. In other words, instead of driving the play to the outside, which is normal, I had them driving it inside, *toward* the goal and not away from it. That way, my forwards could be looking at their defensemen at all times and be ready for a pass or loose puck. You had to have a great defense to play like that, and we had it.

"That team had no weakness at all, even when I was carrying seven rookies for a while. Why, three of those rookies—Frankie Brimsek, Jack Crawford and Roy Conacher—were among our best men. They put the finishing touches on a good team and made it a great one."

The Bruins were great enough to win games with Schmidt and Cowley, their two top centers, out with injuries. They won with 40-year-old Ralph (Cooney) Weiland filling in at center although he was long past his peak year of 1929 when he scored a team record 73 points. They won with Dit Clapper, a ten-year star at forward, who had shifted to defense. They won with the aged and battered Eddie Shore playing his next-to-last season and the kid goalie Frankie Brimsek playing his first.

The Bruins began their dynasty in 1938–39 with a first line of Bill Cowley, Ray Getliffe and Charlie Sands. The second line was the youthful Krauts playing their second full season. Gordie Pettinger centered the third line for Roy Conacher and Mel Hill, who was to earn a new name, "Sudden Death," in the drama of a playoff later that season.

On defense stood the still awesome Shore and Clapper, the team's "cop." "A lot of us were little guys," says Milt Schmidt, "but none of us were afraid to get into scraps. We were very brave—all because we had Dit Clapper on our side." The other defensemen were Johnny Crawford and Flash Hollett. In goal was the dependable veteran Cecil (Tiny) Thompson.

As the 1938–39 season began Art Ross was mulling over in his mind what to do about Thompson. In the previous season Ross had brought up a young goalie to fill in for the injured Tiny, the dark-haired and handsome Frankie Brimsek. He was one of those rarities in the NHL—he was born in the United States. A refugee from the frigid prairie winters of Eveleth, Minn., Brimsek had a quickness of hands that astonished Ross. Now Ross was wondering: Was this kid, Brimsek, a better goalie than Tiny Thompson?

What spurred Ross to decide between the two was an offer from Detroit: The Red Wings would pay $15,000, a goodly sum in those depression days, for Thompson. Ross came to a decision. He sold Thompson to the Wings and brought up Brimsek from Providence as his No. 1 goalie.

The Bruin players reacted angrily. Dit Clapper threatened to quit. "How could you give up someone who's been the league's top goaltender for four seasons and replace him with a kid?" Clapper snapped at Ross. "The team took it pretty badly," Milt Schmidt remembers. "We just couldn't understand Mr. Ross replacing a sure thing with a rookie."

The Bruin fans were just as upset. In a letter to a sports editor one fan pointed out that Brimsek was of Slavic ancestry. "Slavs don't have the temperament to be goalies," he wrote. Fans disliked Brimsek's way of standing still and not reacting until the last split-second to a shot. "A good goalie just doesn't stand there," one fan complained. And in the

Mel Hill in 1938: Ahead there was Sudden Death.

taverns around Boston Garden you heard grumbling about Brimsek being U.S. born. "It takes," pontificated one fan over his beer, "a good Canadian to stop a good Canadian."

Brimsek quickly hushed the critics. First of all, the fans were amused by his superstitious habit of wearing an old pair of red pants over his Bruin uniform. And they gradually got to appreciate the way he planted his 5–foot–9, 170-pound body like a rock at the cage mouth, using hands as quick as a pickpocket's to pluck off flying pucks. In Brimsek's first game the Boston fans whistled appreciatively when he blanked the Black Hawks, 2–0. They were cheering his name after his next game when he turned in another shutout. And the fans and writers were calling him Mr. Zero after he blanked the Rangers, 3—0, for his third straight shutout. When the Canadiens—ah, who else?—broke his shutout streak after 231 minutes and 54 seconds of goaltending, the Garden fans rose and paid him a minute of tribute with their cheering.

Frankie promptly went on another streak, Boston winning successive shutouts, 1–0, 2–0 and 3–0. Finally, on Christmas Day before some 16,000 screeching fans at the Boston Garden, the Rangers' Phil Watson slammed in a goal to end the streak and beat the Bruins, 1–0; it was the first goal against Brimsek in 220 minutes of hockey.

The Rangers went away impressed. "He's as quick as a cat," coach Lester Patrick said after the game. "Trying to get him to make the first move is like pushing over Washington Monument."

Those were about the only kind words exchanged between the Rangers and their old rivals, the Bruins, during that 1938–39 season. The emotional rivalry, always simmering, had flamed during the season as the Rangers trailed the Bruins in the race for first place, the Rangers finishing second, 16 points behind the Bruins, who had a 36–10–2 record. On the eve of the opening-round playoffs, a best-of-seven series between the two clubs, angry words bounced back and forth. Art Ross ridiculed the "streamlined" passing attack of the quick Rangers as "lightweight." Lester Patrick called the Bruins "dirty players" because of their bruising intimidation of opponents.

The first game was played at New York's Madison Square Garden. Early in the game the Rangers' Alex Shibicky blasted the puck by Brimsek, but Bill Cowley tied it with a shot that whizzed by Davey Kerr. The teams went into overtime tied 1–1. For the millions of Boston and New York fans, this sudden-death game would be a preview of the entire stomach-wrenching series.

The two teams battled through the 20-minute overtime without a goal being scored. The ice was recoated and the teams struggled through another overtime. Each team was playing defensive hockey now, guarding its ice with care while looking for a mistake that could be turned into a break-away score.

At the start of the third overtime—it was now close to 1 o'clock in the morning, the fans limp from yelling, the players white-faced with exhaustion—the Bruins huddled near their bench. Art Ross looked at center Bill Cowley. "They've got Conacher covered," Ross said in his rasping growl. "Feed Hill."

Cowley stared, his eyes showing his surprise. Rightwinger Mel Hill had knocked in only ten goals all season long. But Cowley nodded. Ross made sense. The Rangers had stuck close to Conacher all night.

Late in that third overtime period Cowley took the puck and angled across the Ranger cage into the corner, pursued by the lumbering Muzz Patrick. Big Muzz aimed a body check at Cowley, but he was too late getting to the quick center. Several other Rangers circled Conacher. Mel Hill slipped between them and veered in front of the cage. Cowley passed the puck to the slender Hill, who slapped it by Davey

Kerr into the cage. The time was 1:10 in the morning, the day after the game had started, and the Bruins were 2–1 winners.

Two days later the two teams clashed again in Boston, and again they struggled into another sudden death overtime, tied 2–2. And again there was Mel Hill, taking a pass from Cowley some 40 feet out, and whisking it in'o the cage. The Bruins had won, 3–2, and now led the series two games to none.

The Bruins easily won the third game, 4–1, and returned to New York dreaming of sweeping the Rangers in four straight. But the feisty Rangers got a lift when Muzz Patrick broke Eddie Shore's nose in a free-for-all and won, 2–1, to send the teams back to Boston.

Writing in SPORT, Lee Greene described the fifth game this way:

"The fifth game, in Boston, was a continuation of the fourth. The teams belted each other from the opening faceoff and both Conacher and Hollett limped to the bench with in-juries. Boston fans showered the Rangers with firecrackers, eggs, oranges and tin cans as the game ended in a 1–1 tie. This time the Rangers got the sudden-death goal, Clint Smith hitting at 17:14 of the overtime period."

The Rangers also won the next game, 3–1, tying the series at three games apiece. On the night of April 2 in Boston the two teams lined up for the faceoff of the seventh and decisive game, some 16,981 fans filling the Garden with their roaring.

Again, incredibly, for the fourth time in seven games, the teams battled each other into sudden-death overtime, then a second overtime, then a third, tied 1–1, and knowing that at any second one shot could put them out of the playoffs. While fans stood and twisted their crumpled programs with wet hands, the players on both sides shot up and down the ice, drenched in sweat, panting, reaching down inside themselves for one more bit of energy.

Halfway through that third period the old man, Eddie Shore, seized the puck and snapped it to Roy Conacher. Roy slammed the puck at the Ranger goalie, Bert Gardiner, who had replaced the injured Kerr earlier in the series. Gardiner grabbed the puck and flipped it to the side to be retrieved by a Ranger. But the deceptively fast Bill Cowley raced to the corner and got to the puck first. He turned and saw Mel Hill veering toward the side of the cage. He passed the puck to Hill, who rammed it by the surprised Gardiner. From that night on, to Bruin fans, Mel Hill would always be "Sudden Death" Hill. His third sudden-death goal had won the game, 2–1, and the series.

After such drama the finals of the Stanley Cup could only be an anti-climax. The Bruins easily whipped the Maple Leafs in five games and carried the Stanley Cup off the rink, winning it ten years after their first. Ahead seemed to stretch a winning dynasty for this team that brimmed over with talent. But in Europe in that year of 1939, Hitler's troops were marching, Panzer tanks were rolling, a war beginning that would shatter this first Great Boston Scoring Machine.

Chapter IX

1940 TO 1958: THE BRUINS RIDE
A ROLLER COASTER

"Can't miss. A sure thing for a second-straight Stanley Cup."

"Well, I don't know. The Rangers are tough, mighty tough. They finished in second place, right behind us. And now we're going into a playoff for the first time without Eddie Shore."

"But the Bruins finished ahead of them, that's the important thing, even without Shore. We'll beat the Rangers in the playoffs."

You heard a lot of conversations like that around Causeway Street and in North Station in the spring of 1940. The 1939—40 Stanley Cup playoffs were about to begin, the second place Rangers matched against the first place Bruins. After the first three games, the Bruins led two games to one. It seemed that the Bruins would win that second straight Cup. But the Rangers rallied to win the next three games and take the series, four games to two. The New Yorkers roared right on to sweep by Toronto and win the Cup.

Art Ross and his Bruins said loudly, "The Bruins will be back." And back they came in 1940–41, winning 27, losing only 8 and tying 13. They nipped the Leafs in seven games, then hustled the Red Wings out of the finals in four games. The Krauts and Frankie Brimsek, Dit Clapper and Bill Cowley, "Sudden Death" Hill and Jack Crawford, the team that may have been Boston's greatest, had won another Stanley Cup—its second in three years.

In 1941–42 the Bruins finished third, well behind the Rangers, but now the team was crumbling as 15 Bruins went off to enlist in the Canadian armed forces and Frankie Brimsek joined the U.S. Coast Guard. Without the Krauts, the Bruins still managed to struggle by Chicago in the 1941–42 playoffs before losing in the semi-finals to Detroit. During the remainder of the war years the Bruins finished no higher than second, but twice scrambled into the playoff finals, losing both times.

For the 1945–46 season the Krauts came marching home, along with Frankie Brimsek, Roy Conacher and Bill Cowley. Dit Clapper was now a playing-coach, with Art Ross a full-time general manager. Clapper and Ross tried to mix their older players with a crop of younger ones like Ferny Flaman, Bep Guidolin, and Don Gallinger. But the Bruins climbed only once as high as second during the last half of the Forties. In 1949–50 they dropped all the way to fifth, winning only 22 games. Dit Clapper suddenly quit as a coach, standing up at a team dinner and saying he was through, ending some 25 years as a Bruin. He was replaced by George (Buck) Boucher, a minor-league coach. One of the first moves by Ross and Boucher was to trade Brimsek to Chicago. The Bruins had high hopes, Ross said, that a young ex-collegian, Jack Gelineau, would make Bostonians forget all about Mr. Zero.

Jack Gelineau didn't make anyone forget Mr. Zero, although he was the Rookie of The Year in 1950. The defense was leaky, the Bruin attack insipid. Suddenly the once-proud Bruins were the door mats of the league. Opposing teams relished coming to Boston Garden for easy victories. But NHL owners began to look coldly at the dwindling crowds in the Garden. At several games only 5,000 or so rattled around in the Garden, their shouts echoing in the emptiness.

The Boston treasury was being drained of dollars. The Boston Garden Corporation, long the "landlord" of the Bruins, decided to try to save the team. The Boston Garden bought control of the Bruins from Weston W. Adams, the son of the team's founder, Walter F. Adams. Walter Brown, president of the Garden, took over as president of the Bruins. As part of the deal, Weston Adams exchanged some of his Bruin stock for stock in the Boston Garden. Subsequently he bought more Garden stock and became one of the largest owners of Garden stock. In the early 1960s, when Walter Brown died, Weston W. Adams again took over as president of the Bruins. His son, Weston (Westy) Adams, Jr., later succeeded him as president, with the senior Adams becoming the chairman of the board.

The new coach, Buck Boucher, survived only a year. He was replaced in 1950 by an ex-Ranger who had long been a burr in the Bruin tail: Lynn Patrick. He came to the Bruins as head coach but with the understanding he would take over as general manager. Art Ross, the old GM, was feuding with Weston Adams and was gradually being eased out of the Bruin front office.

One of Patrick's first moves was to acquire "Wild Bill" Ezinicki in a trade with the Maple Leafs. Though Wild Bill, an aging forward, could not make the team a winner, he did give the Bruins their old punishing authority. For years, ever since they had battled in junior hockey, he and Detroit's Ted Lindsay had been winging punches at one another. During a game early in 1951, the two slashed at each other with their sticks. Then, dropping sticks and gloves, they barreled into each other, fists flying. Lindsay whapped a series of punches into Wild Bill's face, knocking him onto the ice.

Wild Bill rarely lost this kind of punch-out. He jumped up and waded in at Lindsay. Two officials grabbed Wild Bill by the arms and as they clamped Bill's arms to his sides, the unimpeded Lindsay whaled away at Wild Bill's face, one crunching blow to the jaw knocking Ezinicki unconscious.

His teammates dragged Wild Bill off the ice. "Why did they keep me away?" Ezinicki said mournfully in the clubhouse. Lindsay had broken Wild Bill's nose and cut his face so badly that surgeons used 19 stitches to close all the cuts.

But the fight had served notice on the league: Beware of Wild Bill when you come to Boston, even if the other Bruins are not as big and bad as of old. Art Ross summed up the sentiments of the league when he said, "I've seen courageous guys in this game, but this Ezinicki beats them all."

In the 1951-52 season the Bruins forged into contention right from the start. But the fans still were staying away from the games. In a game in December, 1951, as Stan Fischler notes in his book, *Bobby Orr and the Big Bad Bruins,* only 4,888 fans attended—and that game was against No. 1 rival New York. The crowd was the thinnest to attend a Bruin game in 17 years. That season the Bruins finished fourth, qualifying for the playoffs but lost in the opening round to the Canadiens, four games to three.

At the start of the 1952-53 season Lynn Patrick thought he had assembled a respectable team. He installed Jim Henry, an old Ranger and Black Hawk, in the nets, replacing Jack Gelineau, who never attained the promise of his rookie year. The two old Krauts, Dumart and Schmidt, were on the wings and Bill Quackenbush headed the defense. Patrick had no hot-handed scorer—the team's leading scorer, Flem Mackell, ranked tenth in the league—but the Bruins squeaked into third place. In the opening round of the playoffs they faced Detroit's hot Red Wings, featuring the lea-

After the 1970-71 season, Johnny Bucyk, "The Chief," was the all-time
Bruins' leader in games played, in assists and also in points scored.

gue's leading scorer, Gordie Howe, and his linemates, Lindsay and Alex Delvecchio. The league's top goalie was Detroit's Terry Sawchuk. "Nobody but nobody," wrote Boston *Record-American* reporter D. Leo Monahan, "figured to knock off Detroit that year."

Lynn Patrick was doing some scheming. He knew he couldn't match the firepower of the Howe-Lindsay-Delvecchio line with any of his lines. So he decided he would try to clamp a Blanket Line on the Detroit high-scoring Production Line, using his Blanket Line to check rather than try to score. He told his Blanket Line, Schmidt, Dumart and Joe Klukay: "Shadow them wherever they go. If Lindsay or Howe go to the bathroom, go with them."

The strategy blew up in Patrick's face in the opening game. The Red Wings demolished the Bruins, 7–0. Patrick stuck to his game plan. "I've got to give this plan one more try," he told the Boston writers. "One game isn't enough time to put in a new system."

In the second game the Boston Blanket Line jammed up the Detroit Production Line, and without the usual scoring from Lindsay, Howe and Delvecchio, the Bruins won, 5–3.

The third game, played in the Boston Garden, went into sudden-death overtime, tied 1–1. For many in the big crowd watching this game, there were memories of 1939 and "Sudden Death" Hill, the fans standing and roaring as the Bruins stood off the heavily favored Wings.

Detroit's Terry Sawchuk was blocking shot after shot as the Bruins stormed in on him. "Shoot higher," one Bruin yelled at Boston winger Jack MacIntyre during a break in the action. "You can beat Sawchuk with the high shot."

MacIntyre nodded. With some 12 minutes gone in sudden death he snared the puck near mid-ice, scooted across the blue line and suddenly slapped at the puck. It sailed off on a rising line, a blackish blur that flashed by Sawchuk's elbow and clanged into the iron bar at the rear of the cage.

Goal! The Bruins had won, 2–1, in overtime, just as they had won in the days of "Sudden Death" Hill and the Krauts. The Boston crowd stood and roared, then stormed happily out of the Garden into the frigid darkness of Causeway Street, talking excitedly about these new come-from-behind Bruins. As Stan Fischler later noted, "If any one game could be credited with starting the hockey revival in Boston, it was [that] contest . . ."

The Bruins went on to knock the Red Wings out of the playoffs, Dumart and Schmidt handcuffing Lindsay and Howe. Now the Bruins entered the finals against a Canadien team that seemed distinctly weaker than Detroit, a young goaltender, Jacques Plante, in the Montreal nets.

But the ballooning hopes of Boston fans for another Stanley Cup began to hiss air when Jim Henry hurt his leg and was replaced by minor-league goaltender Gordon "Red" Henry. Rocket Richard and Elmer Lach rained rubber at the rookie and wiped out the Bruins in five games.

But now the huge crowds again were streaming into Boston Garden to watch the Bruins. And the Bruins made periodic thrusts toward the top. In 1954, after retiring as a player, Milt Schmidt took over as coach, with Lynn Patrick becoming the full-time general manager. The still-crusty Art Ross, after some 25 years as head of the Bruin front office, went into a quiet retirement in a Boston suburb.

Schmidt and Patrick still lacked the one or two high scorers a contender must have. The fiery Leo Labine, their best shooter, never ranked among the top half-dozen NHL scorers. But Patrick and Schmidt strengthened the defense in 1955 by obtaining goalie Terry Sawchuk, almost impenetrable when he wasn't in one of his sulky moods, from Detroit. With Hal Laycoe and Bill Quackenbush solidifying the defense, the Bruins did not yield many easy goals. In 1956–57, after finishing a bad fifth the year before, the Bruins rose to third and blasted the Red Wings out of the opening round of the playoffs. They entered the finals against Montreal, the highest they had climbed in four years, but lost, four games to one.

By 1957–58 Patrick and Schmidt had found the high-scoring line they had been seeking: Johnny (Chief) Bucyk, Bronco Horvath and Vic Stasiuk, the Uke line, so-named because of the trio's Ukranian ancestry. These three, along with two other young shooters, Don McKenney and Jerry Toppazzini, chipped in with 20 or more goals for the next two seasons, and the Bruins were now peppering goalies with a fury that reminded fans of the Dynamite Line of the 20s and the Kraut Line of the 30s. Terry Sawchuk had quit the team after threatening to sue some newspapermen for slander, but ex-Wing Harry Lumley and Don Simmons, up from the minors, were boulders in front of the cage, with Leo Boivin and Doug Mohns sticking out on defense.

In 1957–58 the Bruins finished fourth, defeated the Rangers, and went into another Stanley Cup final against the Canadiens. They battled the Canadiens furiously through six games before bowing, the Canadiens winning their third straight Stanley Cup.

Many experts thought the Bruins were poised to snap that Canadien dynasty as the 1958–59 season started. And the experts' forecasts looked accurate enough as Boston finished second behind Montreal in the regular season. The Bruins were the second highest-scoring team in the league. Don McKenney led with 32 goals, Vic Stasiuk punched in 27, Johnny Bucyk 24, and Jerry Toppazzini 21.

The word was out on Causeway Street: This is the year we stop Les Canadiens. Milt Schmidt talked confidently to reporters: "We've got the guns to score against the Canadiens, even though Jacques Plante is one of the great goalies. But we have got to do a job on Jean Beliveau and Henri Richard."

The Bruins never got a chance to do that job. The lowly

Toronto Maple Leafs, a fourth place below–.500 club, upset them in seven games, knocking them out of the playoffs and the Canadiens then beat Toronto to win the fourth of their five straight Stanley Cups.

The Boston Bruins would not rise again until all the members of that team, Johnny Bucyk excepted, were long gone. The years of losing—and losing, and losing—were about to begin.

Chapter X

THE FANS

"WE SHALL OVERCOME"

We were walking through North Station on the way to the Boston Garden on this wintry afternoon in 1966—John Havlicek, the Boston Celtic star, and I. I saw a long line of people waiting to buy tickets at the Garden box office. "You're going to have a big crowd for the game tonight," I said to Havlicek.

"Naw," Havlicek said, frowning. "They're here to buy tickets for the hockey game."

He was right. That night there were fewer than 8,000 people in the Garden to watch a basketball doubleheader— and an excellent doubleheader at that: New York against Philadelphia, Boston against Los Angeles.

The next night a capacity crowd of some 15,000 filled the Garden to watch the Bruins, who hadn't made the playoffs in seven years, meet the Red Wings in a meaningless game;

the Red Wings were a sorry fifth in the league and the Bruins an even sorrier sixth.

All through those eight depressing years when the Bruins were the whipped curs of the league—finishing next to last twice and last six times—the crowds flooded into Boston Garden to see them play. While the team was finishing in last place for the fourth year in succession in 1963–64, attendance leaped by some 30,000 over the previous year. In one season the last place Bruins outdrew the Red Wings, who went on to the Stanley Cup finals. Year-in and year-out the Bruins pulled in bigger crowds than the world champion Celtics, who won more championships than any team in history.

Why are Bruin fans so loyal? What draws them to the Bruins in good years or bad?

Look at their faces as they stream down Causeway Street to the Garden on hockey night. They are white, middle-class faces, many of them ruddied by the cold. They like beer and hamburgers and steak with potatoes, and they like wrestling and the Red Sox. For years they rooted for the pro football Giants, but now they go to Patriot games, and before they married and moved to the suburbs, they nearly always went to the fights. They don't care for the Beatles, but they like Elvis and Sinatra and Johnny Cash. Their parents grew up in neighborhoods like Dorchester, where some of them still live, but most own small-lawned houses in suburbs like Lynn and Revere. They wear American flags in their lapels and worry about kids using dope. They talk about the war in Viet Nam, rising taxes, the welfare mess, school busing—and the Bruins.

They can be as critical of the Bruins as they can be of higher taxes. I stood among them as we watched the Canadiens beat the Bruins in that seventh game of the 1970–71 season. At the intermissions, the Bruins trailing, they crowded the staircases, draining paper cups of beer and seeming to

Two Bruins' goalies—the immortal Mr. Zero, Frankie Brimsek, and Gerry Cheevers, who shares the position today with Ed Johnston.

sense the outcome. "Tom Johnson is nothing but Milt Schmidt's lapdog," one man, about 25 and tieless, is telling someone else. Another is saying to a friend: "When did this team ever win a big one, I ask you?" One woman is saying loudly to her date: "A bunch of fat cats, that's all they are, them with their $400,000 salaries." One tall, thin man in horn-rimmed glasses, maybe a year or two out of college, sees my press tab and snaps at me angrily: "Interview me. I'll tell you what's wrong with this team . . ." The knuckled fist whitens as he shakes it in front of my face. They are physical, these Bruin fans, very physical.

But then the game resumes and the fans are back in their seats, roaring for Orr and Espy and McKenzie, cheering every Bruin attack. When the last minute begins to wind down, there is no booing, only a numbed quiet as the truth beats painfully on the heart: *The Bruins, the Bruins good Lord, the Bruins are going to lose.*

They trudge quietly out of the Garden, some still muttering but in hushed tones, like mourners at a funeral. One man, about 35, sums up the philosophical way these fans have come to accept the good and the bad from the Bruins over nearly half a century. "It's all over but history," he says, and in his own way he has made clear his resigned acceptance.

What first strikes you, looking at the Bruin fans crowded into the Garden, is the remarkable percentage who are women—perhaps as many as one in four, the highest percentage I have ever seen at any sports event, horse racing possibly excepted. They come in twos and threes, or they come with dates or husbands. The teenagers are dressed in bleached levis or in boots and minis, the women in minis or pants suits. They are not the blank-faced female spectators that you see at baseball and basketball games. They come to stand and scream, hands cupped over their red lips, their shrill cries cutting through the clamor of the Garden: "Get a haircut Bobby, why don't you?" And over and over in the fury of a Boston power play: "Kill 'im, Teddy, kill 'im, kill 'im . . . "

That is the common denominator of all the Bruin fans: aggressiveness. They are aggressive themselves in the way they taunt the Bruins and opposing players, hanging high in the balcony over the ice, as though they were perched on one of those second-story walk-up porches in a Dorchester tenement, screaming at the kids down in the street. They literally howl into the ears of the Bruins, and it is this ability to communicate with the players, I suspect, that adds to the I-am-a-part-of-the-action fervor of a Bruin fan.

One also suspects, talking to them, that many or most of them relished contact sports—hockey, football and wrestling —when they were younger, as participants or spectators. Most have an aggressive, assertive, even cocky way of talking and acting.

They want their heroes to be the same way: the brawling Turk, the rampaging McKenzie, the fiercely checking Orr. One of the team's best scorers during the lean years of the early Sixties was Don McKenney. But he was never popular with Bruin fans and after McKenney was traded a Bruin official explained why to Stan Fischler: "He just wouldn't mix it up in the corners."

A Bruin fan's kind of guy is goalie Ed Johnston. I recall a game in 1971 in which Johnston was beaten on a long shot. A minute later someone hit a dribbler that he scooped up. The crowd let out a mock cheer. Johnston raised his stick in an obvious gesture. The fans laughed and burst into applause. This was their kind of humor, their kind of a response, their kind of a man.

A Toronto writer, Peter Gzowski, observed the Bruin fans during the Sixties when the team once went 22 games without a victory. Wrote Gzowski: "Boston fans seem to want to win all right, but winning just doesn't seem as important as it does in other cities—and certainly not as important as some

good rough bodychecks . . . Win or lose, Boston fans seem to get more fun out of hockey than fans in any other city. But they like their hockey simple, and as tough as possible."

Toronto *Telegram* sports editor Scott Young once wrote: "No doubt they (Bruin fans) are nice people when at home or at church. In Boston Garden they become a Dracula of a crowd, with an unslakeable thirst."

The Bruin fans flaunt their bloodthirsty reputation. At every game they post the same banner as a warning to a particular visiting player or coach. The banner reads: RE-MEMBER THAT LADY BYNG DIED IN BOSTON. The Boston Garden, that banner is saying, is no place for the gentlemanly hockey player. Once I overheard two Bruin fans discussing an incident that had happened earlier in the season: a fan in Chicago had thrown a tin can that hit Phil Esposito on the head.

"That was a terrible thing," one fan said, obviously serious. "Of course, Phil *was* a visiting player . . ."

One Bruin who delighted the fans as soon as he put on the gold and black of the Bruins in 1961 was Ted Green. In one of his first games as a Bruin, a meaningless exhibition game against Toronto, Ted started a wild free-for-all in which he broke a hand pounding it on Bob Nevin's skull. Terrible Teddy, as he was soon called, tried to lift up the Bruins with the force of his own steely-eyed personality. But the years of losing began to deaden the club. Too many of the players had become infected with a cynical what's-the-use? attitude as the Bruin front office wheeled and dealed players, coaches and even general managers in a frantic effort to turn the team around and start it ascending to the top instead of sinking to the bottom each season.

Lynn Patrick went, Hap Emms coming in as general manager. Phil Watson succeeded Milt Schmidt as coach. But Watson didn't last long, Milt Schmidt coming back to take over as coach.

The silver-haired Schmidt struggled to remake the team into a winner. But there were uncounted nights when he awoke in the dark and could not sleep, tortured by the weaknesses of the team. "People tell me to forget it, to forget my worries," he once told a friend. "How the heck can I forget them? They're there all the time—they're my worries—and I've got to do something about them.

"The trouble is keeping the guys up, keeping them interested. With our kind of hockey team, in last place almost every year, you can get down pretty quick. I've got to keep brainwashing, brainwashing, brainwashing. Sometimes I chew them out, other times I go easy. You can't have a defeatist attitude and I've got to fight it all the time."

There was nothing defeatist, however, in the hopes and dreams of the loyal Bruin fans during their team's eight-year stay in the NHL's bottom. Once, as the Canadiens were piling up a big lead while skating right over the smaller Bruins, a few fans began to sing, the volume thin and reedy at first. But then more and more people joined in the singing, the voices of a choir of 15,000 soon swelling across the Garden, the Bruin fans looking to the future as they sang, *We Shall Overcome.*

Chapter XI

OH, THE LOVELIEST OF HEADACHES

The warm May sun, streaking through the El structure on Causeway Street, traced grill patterns on the walls of Milt Schmidt's office. This was the early spring of 1967. A few weeks earlier he had been appointed general manager of the Bruins, replacing Hap Emms. In the previous season Milt had again given up the coaching job, handing it over to Harry Sinden, who had been the coach of the Bruin farm team in Oklahoma City. A former defenseman, Sinden, only 35, had a reputation for being a crafty tactician and an explosive and inspirational leader.

Sitting at his desk, Milt glumly scanned the record of that 1966–67 Bruin season. The Bruins had won only 17 games, finishing dead-last in the NHL, their eighth successive year banished from the playoffs. No team in NHL history had been out of the playoffs so long, and in Boston and around the league people were calling the situation an out-and-out disgrace.

"For sure we can't stand pat," Schmidt was telling a friend, grinning slightly. "What we have got to do is to get some of those big forwards, like the ones we once had, the size of a Dit Clapper or a Woody Dumart."

Harry Sinden was thinking much the same thoughts. "The 1966 team lacked size," he told Sports Illustrated's Mark Mulvoy. "Most of the players were under 5–10, and small players never do well in the corners or around the net, the places where hockey games are won and lost."

That 1966 team did have Bobby Orr, however, the wonder-boy who had come to the NHL acclaimed as the greatest player ever to come out of junior hockey. Bobby had proved he was every bit as great as those press notices by winning the Calder Trophy as the NHL's rookie of the year. But Schmidt and Sinden knew that Bobby Orr alone could not lift this team of losers onto the pathway toward a Stanley Cup.

In his office Schmidt was looking at three names on the roster of the Chicago Black Hawks. The names were: Phil Esposito listed at 6–1 and 198 pounds; Fred Stanfield, 5–10 and 182 pounds; and Ken Hodge, 6–foot–2 and 206 pounds. Ever since the Stanley Cup playoffs a month earlier, Milt had been talking to Chicago general manager Tommy Ivan about these three big forwards, the kind he wanted up front for Boston. Ivan had mentioned the names of three Boston players: the 155-pound Boston center, Pit Martin; Gilles Marotte, a highly acclaimed defenseman; and minor-league goaltender Jack Norris.

Milt knew that Tommy Ivan had been casting sour glances at Phil Esposito, his center, after Phil's second successive poor playoff. And Milt also knew that Stanfield and Hodge were unhappy with their salaries and low ice-time in Chicago, where most of the money and the action were going to Bobby Hull and Stan Mikita.

Schmidt was not at all sure that Esposito, Hodge and Stanfield could help the Bruins. All three were too young and

Already, Bobby **Orr** has won more awards in hockey than anyone except for Gordie Howe. And Bobby still has most of his career ahead.

relatively untested for him to be positive of their true quality. But all three were big, and at this desperate point in Bruin history, all Schmidt wanted were big bodies.

Time, however, was running out on a trade. By May 15 all NHL teams had to freeze their rosters. Now it was around 3 o'clock on May 15, Schmidt wondering if he should make a move or wait to hear from Ivan.

Milt's phone rang. Calling from Florida was Tommy Ivan. "I'm down here for a few days, Milt," Tommy said, "and I thought I'd let you know my telephone number."

Milt jotted down the number. He thought for several more hours. He had never realized how much was involved in a trade. Now, in his first month as a general manager, he had to decide on giving up an outstanding center and a promising defenseman for three hulking young forwards.

Finally, he decided he had to do it. Milt got Ivan on the phone and the three-for-three deal was made. That fall of 1967, at the London, Ontario, training camp of the Bruins, as Harry Sinden said three years later, "the modern-day Boston Bruins—the Big Bad Bruins as everybody later called us—was born."

For the first time as a Bruin coach, Sinden could establish season-long lines. Esposito centered one, with Hodge and the veteran Ron Murphy on the wings. Stanfield centered the other, with Johnny Bucyk and Johnny McKenzie the wingers.

In that camp there was a surprise: a tough 21-year-old battler, Derek Sanderson, whom everybody called Turk. Derek popped all the way from the seventh line at the training camp to the third line, centering a line with the veteran Eddie Westfall and the hard-nosed Eddie Shack, obtained in a trade with Toronto, on the wings.

"Derek gave me a few headaches because of his tardiness for practice," Sinden said later that season, "and sometimes I had to provide him with a tie to wear when we were traveling, but on the ice he gave 100 percent and became the best faceoff man in the NHL."

On defense Sinden paired the burly Don Awrey with the smaller Teddy Green. Up until then Awrey had been far from the meanest defenseman in the NHL. But playing with Green he had to get tougher or feel the sting of Green's tongue—and maybe his fists. "In the past I wasn't as aggressive as I should have been," Awrey told Stan Fischler. "I did talk things over with Teddy Green. I'll tell you something: Just knowing I have him to back me up helps a lot . . . All I can tell you is that things have changed on this club. In years past if somebody got into a scrap, one or two might join in. Now, on this club, anybody's fight is everybody's fight. That's the way it is."

Bobby Orr paired off with Dallas Smith. The two goaltenders were Gerry Cheevers and Ed Johnston. "You know," Johnston once said, "Gerry and I should give part of our salaries to Orr. The kid blocks almost as many shots as we do." "He blocks more," snapped Phil Esposito.

At the training camp each Bruin began to feel a sense of confidence growing inside him, like a football being inflated. If they worked together as a unit, they began to tell each other, they could be winners. Yes, *winners*. Phil Esposito told them so, in talk after talk, and Phil had played with winners, hadn't he? He should know.

Bobby Orr, though only a second-year man, helped in his quiet way to bring the team together. For a week or so two of the Bruins had been feuding, and Bobby realized that if the arguing went on, the team would be split into factions. One day a grinning Bobby loudly invited the two feuding players to come to the center of the clubhouse. "You have your choice of weapons for a duel," Bobby said, snickering. He pulled from a paper bag a pair of miniature boxing gloves, a tiny cannon, a rubber knife and a water pistol.

As he pulled each item out of the bag, the players roared.

Soon the two players, who had been grimly staring at each other, were leaning back and laughing, and the feud was over.

Over and over, at each practice session, Harry Sinden tried to imbue the team with his aggressive hit-hit-hit philosophy. "My theory," he told the players, "is to keep the puck in the other team's zone. If you do that you force mistakes that can be converted into goals. But you have to be forechecking all the time. You can't stop hitting."

Team spirit began to grow. "I've been on a lot of teams," said the much-traveled Johnny McKenzie, "and I've never seen one with spirit like this." One player scrawled THINK KILL on the clubhouse mirror. The rookie brawler, Derek Sanderson, waded into the Rangers' Orland Kurtenbach, considered the best boxer in the league, and fist-fought him to a bloody draw. Teddy Green kayoed another Ranger, Larry Jeffrey, then stood over his prostrate body and raised his stick, daring another Ranger to approach him. None did. The Bruin players joked about how certain players avoided the puck against the Bruins, fearful of being drawn and quartered.

Sports Illustrated published an article by Pete Axthelm titled: "Bobby Orr and the Animals," and it said of the Big Bad Bruins: "They have changed from a small meek team that often appeared to be going through the motions into a brawling, powerful unit good enough to lead the league."

The Bruins climbed from sixth to third in that 1967–68 season and faced the Canadiens in their first Stanley Cup round in eight years. Stan Fischler has written that the years of losing left "an indelible scar on those who suffered through" those depression years of the Sixties. The memory of all those losses, Fischler said, "contaminated them (the Bruins) in big games during the 1967–68 and 1968–69 play-off seasons." Harry Sinden has said that "we simply were not ready to win the cup." For whatever reasons, the Bruins lost in four straight to the Canadiens in 1967–68.

The next season they stood at the top of the Eastern Division for most of the season. Then Green and Orr were hurt and they lost first place and the Prince of Wales trophy to Montreal on the last weekend of the season. But they brushed by Toronto in four games and went into the finals against Les Canadiens, who were seeking their second-straight cup.

In the first two games the Bruins led with only 90 seconds remaining. In both games the Canadiens shoved across the tying goal and went on to win in overtime. The Bruins did not wilt, fighting back to win the next two games to tie the series at two games apiece. But Montreal triumphed in the fifth game to lead, three games to two.

In the sixth game the two teams were tied after three periods. They were still tied after the first 20-minutes of sudden-death overtime. But this time there was no Mel Hill lurking around the crease to slap in a game-ending shot for the Bruins. Instead Jean Beliveau rammed in the game-winner for the Canadiens to win the Stanley Cup. Of that series Harry Sinden said later, "Those were my most disappointing days as coach."

The team that came out of the London training camp for the start of the 1969–70 season was much the same team that had come together for the first time two years earlier. The only exceptions were Wayne "Swoop" Carleton, who had replaced the departed Eddie Shack on the line with Sanderson and Westfall; Wayne Cashman, who replaced the retired Ron Murphy on the Esposito-Hodge line; and Rick Smith, who replaced Teddy Green, lost for the season after a near-tragic skull fracture.

It was an attack-minded team willing to give up goals as long as it could strafe opposing goalies with 40 or 50 shots a night. With shooters like Esposito, the top scorer the previous season, Orr and the rest, Harry Sinden figured that enough of those shots would go through to win most games.

In that 1969–70 season the Bruins won 40, lost 17, and tied

19 for a total of 99 points, tying the Black Hawks for first place in the Eastern Division. The Hawks were awarded first place, however, because they had won five more games.

In the playoffs the Bruins took on the Rangers in the quarter-finals. Discussing the Rangers one day in the Boston clubhouse, Harry Sinden told the Bruins his game plan: "We have never lost to this team when we played a physical game. We have got to go out there and forecheck their defensemen, because all of them can handle the puck real well. If we hit them hard we can disorganize them before they can start an attack. Also we want to get off as many shots as we can at Ed Giacomin. He looks tired. If we can get enough shots on him, we'll get enough by to win."

In the first two games in Boston the Bruins body checked the Ranger defensemen left, right and everywhere but up into the galleries, and the Bruins won both games. The Ranger defensemen slipped loose in the next two games in New York, however, and the Rangers won both games to even the series at two games apiece.

Back in Boston the Bruins could wing only 28 shots at Giacomin in the fifth game, while the Rangers were raining 34 shots at Gerry Cheevers. But Giacomin made one more mistake than Cheevers and the Bruins won, 3–2.

In the sixth game the Rangers jumped out into a 1–0 lead on a goal by Brad Park, and the crowd of close to 20,000 in the new Madison Square Garden applauded the goal for well over a minute. Then Bobby Orr went to work. He took a pass from Bucyk and scored. On the power play he took a pass from Esposito and scored. It was his sixth goal of the series. The Bruins coasted to a 4–1 victory to win the series, four games to two.

After the series Ranger coach Emile Francis said that Orr had been the difference between the two teams. Harry Sinden tended to disagree. "Orr is always a difference," he said, "because no player in hockey can match him." But Sinden pointed to the statistics which showed that the Rangers had outshot the Bruins in the six-game series, 220–181. "To me," Harry said, "the more important difference was Gerry Cheevers."

The Bruins now advanced to the semi-final round against the Black Hawks, Phil facing Tony in another brother-vs.-brother Stanley Cup confrontation. Again Harry Sinden collected his players in the clubhouse for another meeting on tactics. "Chicago is doing some new things," he told his players, "like playing a very tight defense and doing a lot of backchecking. But what it all comes down to for us is this: To beat the Hawks, we must stop Hull and Mikita."

Sinden assigned the versatile Eddie Westfall to shadow Hull. "Eddie is smart," Sinden later told Mark Mulvoy. "He doesn't aggravate Bobby. He doesn't stay too close to him. He circles around, but always is in position when Hull gets the puck."

The swift-as-a-bug Mikita couldn't be tailed so easily. Sinden assigned his wingers to check Mikita's wingers, so he couldn't pass to the open man, which Mikita likes to do.

With Hull's shooting and Mikita's passing bottled up, Phil Esposito went to work slamming pucks at brother Tony. There are those around the league who insist that Phil knows something about Tony that other shooters don't know. Phil has never admitted to this, but he has always scored well against his brother. In the first game of the playoff he whapped in three of the first four Bruin goals and the Bruins won easily, 6–3. During the entire series Phil whizzed five pucks past Tony and assisted on four other goals as the Bruins routed the Black Hawks in four straight.

Again the Bruins were in the Stanley Cup finals, this time against a new foe: the St. Louis Blues, a new franchise that had dominated the NHL's Western Division, made up entirely of new teams, from 1967 to 1970. This was the third straight trip to the finals by the Blues, who had yet to win a

The Bruins always had a
reputation for ferocious
play. People like Ted Green,
left, a long-time bad boy of
hockey, kept things stewing
all the time. The melee,
above, with bodies thrash-
ing about is typical of the
Bruins.

Bobby Orr, mingling at right with the Canadiens' Jean Beliveau has never backed off from a fight. The author describes the Bruins' music as "the thudding sounds of bodies being whammed against the boards—thump! thump!"

game in the Cup finals against the established eastern teams.

Harry Sinden respected the Blues, who had beaten the Bruins twice in six games during the season. "Their defensemen are big and strong and we will have trouble penetrating on the inside," he told the Bruins. "But they are slow. They're not quick enough to come outside against wingers busting wide, so you centermen pass to the boards."

In the first game the Blues tried to shadow Bobby Orr with a wingman, but that left a gap on the side, and Johnny Bucyk glided through the gap to score three goals in the first game, which Boston won, 6–1.

The Bruins easily won the next two games. On Sunday, May 10, 1971, those loyal Bruin fans, who had dreamed so long of seeing the Stanley Cup come back to Boston, crowded into the old Garden, roaring expectantly when the Bruins paraded onto the ice to tumultuous music for their warmups.

In his tiny office off the Bruin clubhouse, Harry Sinden paced the floor. To a friend he jerked a thumb at a pile of newspapers on his desk. "Those papers make everything look so easy," he growled. "Sure we should win today, but Mr. Glenn Hall is out there today and the puck can take some funny bounces."

Glenn Hall had played in a record 112 Stanley Cup games. And Sinden knew that the Blue shooters would be firing the puck much more loosely than the Bruins, with nothing to lose, down three games to none in the best-of-seven series.

The Bruins scored first but St. Louis' Red Berenson tied the game and the Blues lunged ahead, 2–1, early in the second period. Esposito flicked a shot by Hall late in the period and the two teams went off for the intermission tied, 2–2.

That tie didn't last long into the third period. After 19 seconds Larry Keenan darted the puck by Gerry Cheevers and again St. Louis led, 3–2. The Blues cozied that lead through some 13 minutes of action, and Bruin fans began to despair of seeing the cup won here in Boston. Glenn Hall looked as though he could bat down thunderbolts. The next game would be in St. Louis.

The Bruin fans were standing, beseeching a goal, as Rick Smith collected the puck. He shoveled it up ice to Johnny McKenzie, who slapped it across to Bucyk. The Chief caught Hall off-balance and rammed the puck by him. The score was tied, 3–3, and it stayed that way until the period ended.

And into sudden-death overtime and memories, for some in the stands, of "Sudden Death" Hill. Only thirty seconds had gone by when Orr picked up the puck across the St. Louis blue line. He snapped the puck toward Turk Sanderson in the right corner. Then Bobby took off on one of his quick-accelerating give-and-go dashes for the goal mouth. Sanderson was hugging the puck like a miser near the boards, fending off Blues who were trying to snatch it from him. Out of the corner of his eye Turk saw the blond No. 4 skimming toward the cage, racing at Glenn Hall from the goalie's left side. At the last possible moment Turk bounced the puck toward Orr, who swung at it while racing between a defenseman and Hall. The defenseman tripped Bobby but as Bobby Orr started to soar through the air, his long body flying bullet-like above the ice, he saw the puck hit the back of the cage. And even as he flew—"I thought I was going right out of the arena"—Bobby stuck up his stick, a smile of triumph lighting his face. The Bruins had won the fourth and final game. The Bruins had come back. The Bruins had won the Stanley Cup.

That night the Bruins drank champagne from "that battered old mug," that Stanley Cup they had won again after 29 years of trying. The next day some 150,000 proud and cheering Bostonians lined the down-town streets as a parade of open limousines carried Bobby and Espy, Gerry Cheevers and Swoop and all of them to a ceremony for a city's heroes.

Espy jumps with joy after scoring record-breaking 59th goal.

One girl leaped into Bobby Orr's limousine and kissed him soundly, telling this young man from Parry Sound just what he had done to the people of the big city.

After the champagne and all the celebrating, someone asked Harry Sinden how he felt in the morning.

"I had," said a grinning Harry, "the loveliest headache I've ever had."

Chapter XII

AND THEN THERE CAME SOMEONE
NAMED DRYDEN

IT WAS A GREAT YEAR.. . . AND A GOOD TIME WAS HAD BY ALL.

So Bruin publicity man Herb Ralby noted in the program for the Stanley Cup playoffs in April of 1971. He wrote those words before Montreal abruptly ended that year, but all in all it was a fantastic year. Here is one man's journal of that season:

September 10—The Stanley Cup champions open their training camp at London, Ontario. After one day for physicals, another for picture-taking, the Bruins get down to work on the third day. There are two workouts a day—at 9 a.m. and at 2:30 in the afternoon. All except two players from last year's champions are on hand. The missing ones played minor roles last season: defenseman Gary Doak and center Jim Lorentz. Coming back after missing the entire season is Teddy Green.

October 11—The Bruins open the 1970–71 season at Boston Garden, defeating the Red Wings. The victory is the Bruins' 24th unbeaten game at home, counting last season's playoff games. The record is 28, held by Montreal. The last time the Bruins lost at home was on January 17, a 1–0 loss to Chicago on a bitterly disputed goal.

October 25—Teddy Green scores the first goal of his comeback season. And he scores it at the Garden, where the filled house pours down a two-minute ovation on him. After the game Teddy says, "That ovation turned the corner for me."

October 29—The Bruins arrive in Detroit unbeaten in their first six games of the season. The Red Wings snap the string, winning 5–3.

October 31—The Bruins face off against the Rangers with first place at stake, the Rangers two points ahead. Boston wins, 6–0, and ties for the Eastern lead.

November 1—The Bruins set a record (counting playoff games) of 29 home games without a defeat, blanking Minnesota, 5–0.

November 5—The St. Louis Blues snap the string, beating the Bruins in Boston, 2–0.

November 6—Phil Esposito leads the league in scoring with 19 points in nine games. John McKenzie is second with 16 and Ken Hodge third with 15. Esposito and Hodge lead the league in assists.

December 1—The Bruins are third highest in the league in penalty minutes. But they lead the league in scoring while shorthanded.

December 6—Phil Esposito posts his third hat-trick of the season as the Bruins beat Pittsburgh, 6–3.

December 8—The Bruins have lost only one game of their last 11, but the Rangers hang close, trailing by only a point.

December 9—Esposito leads the league in scoring with 22 goals and 27 assists for 49 points. He is 11 points ahead of his 1968–69 pace when he set the scoring record with 126 points.

In 1970-71 Phil Esposito scored more goals over one season, 76, than any-
one in NHL history. And 16 of the goals won games—also a record.

He loses the lead in assists to Bobby Orr, who now has 28.

December 13—Esposito scores three goals in a game for his fourth hat-trick as the Bruins wreck Detroit at the Garden, 6–2. He is tied for the most hat-tricks in a season with four others: Bobby Hull, Maurice Richard, Jean Beliveau and Frank Mahovlich. Says coach Tom Johnson, who averaged three goals *a season* as a defenseman: "I'm not up on those records."

December 20—The Bruins wallop Minnesota, 7–1, at the Garden. It is their eighth straight victory, their longest winning streak since 1938–39. Yet they lead the Rangers by only two points as New York has lost only one game in the last nine.

December 26—After winning ten straight games, the Bruins lose, 4–2, in Pittsburgh. They were four games short of tying the league record of 14, set by the 1929–30 Boston Bruins.

January 7—The Bruins wallop the Canucks to reach the halfway mark of the season. Phil Esposito is averaging two points a game, well above his own record of 1.7 points a game. He has scored 34 goals and is closing in on Bobby Hull's record of 58. He has 72 points and is fast approaching his own record of 126.

January 8—The Bruins place five men on the 12-man Eastern All-Stars: Orr, Esposito, Hodge, Bucyk and McKenzie. The Rangers put six men on the team, with Montreal contributing the 12th man.

January 12—The Bruins have won 15 of their last 17 games but the Rangers cling like chewing gum to a shoe, trailing by only a single point.

January 14—Esposito collects his fifth hat-trick of the season in a 9–5 victory over Los Angeles at the Garden to set a modern record.

January 22—The Bruins recall 20-year-old Reggie Leach from Oklahoma City. The Bruins' No. 1 choice in the amateur draft last year, he has scored 23 goals in 36 games at Oklahoma City. He replaces the injured McKenzie, out for a month with a shoulder separation.

January 24—On Teddy Green Night the Bruins present him with a 4–2 victory over Montreal.

January 27—The Bruins visit New York to play the Rangers, who trail the Bruins by only three points. The two teams tie, 2–2.

January 28—Don Marcotte knocks in his sixth shorthanded goal of the season and the Bruins have set another record with 15 shorthanded goals in a season.

January 31—The Bruins acquire Mike Walton from Toronto.

February 9—Ken Hodge gets an assist on all six goals in a 6–3 victory over the fading Rangers, and those six assists in one game is a Bruin record.

February 16—Bruins run up an unbeaten string of 12 games before losing 5–4 to the Canucks in Vancouver.

February 25—Bruins crush the Canucks, 8–3, at the Garden, their 22nd home victory without a loss. This is their second crack this season at the Montreal record of 28. The Bruins now lead the second-place Rangers by nine points.

March 4—The Bruins rout the Seals, 7–0, for their 24th straight home victory without a loss. Tom Johnson benches the Esposito-Hodge-Cashman line, the highest-scoring line in history, during the third period to give Bucyk a chance at the hat-trick, and Johnny gets his third goal. "How could he bench us?" Hodge asks in mock anger after the game. "Just proves you can't rest on your laurels," retorts Tomcat.

March 6—The quiet Don Marcotte speaks up, asking that his number be changed from 29 to 21 "because 29 is too heavy to carry." Johnson agrees. "Sure we've got some wacky guts," Tom says, "but that's what it takes."

March 8—Boston sporting goods stores report "fantastic" sales of hockey gear. Rinks in the Boston area are jammed with hockey players who have Walter Mittyish dreams of being Bruins. They range in age from five to 70. But the 70-year-old players have league rules against body-checking.

March 10—Bobby Orr raps in two goals and gets an assist for a season's total of 122 points, breaking his own league record for defensemen, which was 120. The second goal is his 34th, breaking his record of 33. The victory gives the Bruins 105 points, the highest ever by a team in one season.

March 11—And still the records come crashing down. Phil Esposito scores his 59th goal in a 7-2 victory over Los Angeles, breaking Hull's record of 58. Orr assists on three goals, breaking his record for assists (87) by a defenseman.

March 13—Maurice (Rocket) Richard, the former Montreal scoring whiz and now a portly 49, scoffs at the Boston scoring records, attributing them to the weakening of NHL teams as new teams have been added. Retorts Esposito: "The game today is twice as fast as it was in the old days. We're not setting records because of weak opponents. We're doing it because of our overall offensive philosophy. We hit, we get position in front of the net, we shoot, we help each other. Bobby Orr would score 100 points with any team in the world. The rest of us do it because we're on the Bruins. You know what I really think about all the comparisons between our records and the older clubs? I think there's never been a hockey club that could tie our laces."

March 20—The Bruins clinch first place in the East with a 5-3 victory over Philadelphia. After a long 30 years the Prince of Wales trophy returns to Boston.

March 21—Buffalo beats the Bruins for the first time ever, 7-5, snapping the Bruins' unbeaten home record at 27 and their winning streak at 13. This was the second time this season that the Bruins were stopped in trying to break Montreal's record of 28 unbeaten regular-season games at home. A portent of things to come? In the game Ken Hodge gets two assists to boost him over the 100-point mark. He becomes the fourth Bruin this season to score more than 100 points. Up until this season only four players in NHL history had scored more than 100 points.

April 7—The first game of the best-of-seven series against the Canadiens is played in Boston, the usual 14,994 capacity crowd howling for Montreal blood and a Boston victory. Boston has beaten the Canadiens five of six times this season. Montreal has a new goalie, the lanky 6–foot–4 Ken Dryden, a law student only a year out of Cornell. He has played fewer than a dozen NHL games. Bobby Orr beats him at 3:57 of the first period after collaring a pass from Stanfield. Montreal's bad man, John Ferguson, whaps the puck by Cheevers to tie the score, 1–1, early in the second period. Cashman rams the puck through Dryden some eight minutes later and Stanfield raps in another in the third period to give the Bruins the 3–1 victory. Boston had 42 shots, Montreal only 31.

April 8—Another 14,994 lucky people—tickets are being scalped at $50 apiece—crowd the Garden for the second game. The rookie, Dryden, seems helpless facing the Boston big guns and Bruin fans begin to wonder why Canadien coach Al MacNeil doesn't pull him out and replace him with the experienced Rogatein Vachon. In two periods the Bruins fire five pucks by the rookie. First Orr scores, then Teddy Green (everyone going wild over that one), then McKenzie, then Cashman, then Sanderson and with five minutes still remaining in the second period, the Bruins seem runaway winners, ahead 5–1.

Then the unthinkable begins to happen. A goal by Henri Richard and the score is 5–2 at intermission. In the third period the unthinkable happens, falling with a thud in the aisles of the ever-more-quiet Garden. Jean Beliveau scores, then Beliveau again. Yvon Cournoyer steals a pass and slaps the puck by Ed Johnston and suddenly the score is tied, 5–5.

Now Dryden is kicking away everything the Bruins throw

at him. At the 15-minute mark Beliveau digs out the puck in the corner and feeds it to Ferguson up close, and Ferguson scores the fourth Canadien goal of the period to put Montreal ahead, 6–5. A little later Frank Mahovlich skates in on Johnston on a breakaway and raps home another goal that clinches a 7–5 Montreal victory.

The come-from-behind victory, on Boston ice, raises Montreal hopes. "It has got to help our spirit," says Canadien captain Jean Beliveau. He looks down at his 39–year-old legs and says, "I just hope they stand up for a couple of more weeks."

Derek Sanderson sits glum-faced at his locker, thoughtfully twisting his mustache. "That kid Dryden hangs tough," he says. "He could have collapsed after those five goals and given up, but he didn't. If we had beaten them bad tonight, we would have seen Vachon for the rest of the series, but now they'll stay with the kid."

April 10—Excitement in Montreal, people shoulder to shoulder moving down St. Catherine Street to the Forum. But many are not yet in their seats when Esposito, who has promised to shoot more, wings the puck by Dryden at the 29-second mark. Cheevers staves off the attacking Canadiens until four minutes into the second period. Frank Mahovlich sticks the puck by Cheesy for the tying goal and brother Pete assists on a goal by Jacques Laperriere some eight minutes later, the Canadiens leading now 2–1 with the Forum seeming to jump, the roaring is so loud. Dryden will not let that puck pass; he stops 37 compared to only 28 for Cheevers. Early in the third period Frank Mahovlich knocks in his third goal of the playoffs and the Canadiens win, 3–1.

April 11—The Bruins make Monday morning a blue one in Montreal. With Montreal leading 1–0 in the second period, Orr scores, then Mike Walton, and in the third period Bobby slips another one by Dryden. Cournoyer scores to move the Canadiens closer, 3–2, but Cheevers gets tremendous help from his defense—he sees only 28 shots all night—and stops any more scoring by Les Canadiens. With fewer than three minutes left, Montreal gets desperate, makes a mistake and Stanfield scores. With only three seconds left Orr knocks the puck into the net and Boston goes home the 5–2 victor, tying the series at two games apiece.

April 13—Back amid the friendliness of the Garden, the Bruins leap out to an early 3–1 lead on goals by Cashman, Esposito and Walton. The Bruins build that lead to 5–1 in the second period on scores by McKenzie and Westfall. Sipping beers at intermission, the fans recall the second game and talk worriedly about blowing another 5–1 lead. But Cheevers again gets great help from the defense—he has to stop only 27 shots while the Bruins pepper 56 at Dryden. Halfway through the third period, the Canadiens edge closer, 5–3, and a rumble of unhappiness begins to crawl through the crowd. But Bucyk and Hodge each score on breakaways and the Bruins win, 7–3. They lead, three games to two, and need only to split the next two games to erase their long-time tormentors.

April 15—Worried Canadien fans cheer when Pete Mahovlich scores to put the Canadiens out in front, 1–0. But Espy ties the game with his third—and last—goal of the series. Henri Richard puts Montreal ahead, 2–1, but Stanfield ties the game, 2–2, early in the second period. Then comes an explosion that turns the crowd of 18,000 into a pack of frenzied lunatics: Jacques Lemaire scores, J. C. Tremblay scores, Henri Richard scores, Pete Mahovlich scores. The Turk tries to stem the tide with a goal that makes the score 6–3 but it is too little too late. Marc Tardif and Laperriere hurtle two more shots by the numbed Cheevers, who saw 43 hunks of rubber streaking at him tonight, and the Canadiens skate off exultant 8–3 victors. In the losers' clubhouse the Bruins seem stunned and tired.

April 17—On this cloudy Saturday morning in Boston

Tom Johnson calls for a practice session at 9 a.m. Turk comes late, mumbling about setting his alarm clock for nine instead of eight. "This was the only time I've been late this season and now I'm in the doghouse," he says sadly. "But don't worry. I'll show up at two o'clock tomorrow."

Herald Traveler writer Tim Horgan asks trainer Dan Canney what happened two nights earlier against Les Canadiens. "Our guys couldn't get up for that game," Canney says. "This is a strange club. As great as these guys are, they've got to be up to play their best." Horgan suggests the Bruins have some reasons to be up for this seventh game: 1) there is money—$1,500 a player if they lose compared to $7,500 if they go on to win the cup; 2) Pride; 3) Peace, because if they lose, writes Horgan, fans will be asking the Bruins for the next 12 months, "What happened?" Adds Horgan: "And then they'll tell you."

April 18—On this grayish Sunday, the Canadiens arrive first at the Garden, the time a little after noon. They have been staying at a motel outside Boston, its exact name kept secret. Jean Beliveau leads them down a long corridor to their dressing room. "Yes, I am tense," he tells me. "I woke up several times during the night and looked at the ceiling. You wonder how you will do." He smiles. "It is good to be tense because you are more sharp. But you never know how your legs are until you get on the ice. Even then, sometimes . . . " His voice trails off, recalling a thousand hockey games. "I mean, sometimes you feel good and you don't play well." He smiles sadly and shrugs, saying it all about the uncertainties of sport.

The young goalie, Ken Dryden, stops to talk about being a goalie in the seventh game of a Stanley Cup playoff. He woke up several times during the night. "The kind of dreams that goalies have, they woke me up," he says. "They're not really dreams. You suddenly jerk awake, your arms out stiff, like you were blocking a shot."

The Turk: A man who makes his own seasons.

Young Rejean Houle's eyes flicker nervously over my face as we talk. "I did not sleep well," he says with an embarrassed smile. "And I could not put down any breakfast. I hope I will not make a mistake that would cost us the game."

The Bruins file in together. They, too, have stayed at a motel hideaway out of town. "Get 'em," an usher shouts at Turk and Turk says casually over his shoulder, "Nothing to worry about."

I say hello to Phil Esposito. He smiles his sad-eyed smile, shakes my hand and is gone, too tense to speak.

I go off to visit the Bruin fans. In section 12 there is a grandmotherly-looking lady in a pale-blue print dress. "If we don't soften them up early," she is growling, "that Cournoyer will murder us."

The players warm up. Dryden seems as big as a basketball forward standing in front of the cage. His huge painted gloves look like the prehensile claws of some giant bird. The face is a blank mask but I see the eyes blinking.

I stand behind the Bruin bench and watch the Bruins warm up. Their faces are chalky white in the glare of the Garden lights. Ed Johnston watches each Canadien shoot, chewing gum, studying, eyes probing. Espy says something and Orr grins.

The game: At 6:50 Ken Hodge intercepts a pass in front of the Montreal cage and speeds at Dryden, juggling the puck in front of him like someone trying to hold a red-hot coal. He is tripped, but he regains his stride and lofts the puck past Dryden's left elbow. The packed crowd roars and roars and roars . . .

Beliveau goes off for hooking Orr, the fans poised on their seats now, looking for one of those power-play goals by the Bruins. But there are no wham-wham-whamp sounds floating up from the rink, the Bruins not checking the Canadiens into the boards, for the Canadiens are noticeably skating faster and more evasively than the Bruins. The Bruins seem tired, Ken Dryden thinks as he stares at them from behind his mask. *If we can just get ahead of them. . .*

Frank Mahovlich slams in his sixth goal of the series to tie the game and Rejean Houle, making no big mistakes, whips another past Cheevers, the few Canadians in the crowd roaring over and over, "Hooo-leeeee, Hooo-leeee . . ."

Late in the second period Lemaire steals the puck away from Rick Smith. A few seconds later J. C. Tremblay slaps the puck by Cheevers for a 3–1 Montreal lead.

At the start of the third period, only ten seconds gone, Lemaire hustles the puck into the right corner. Cheevers shifts to the right. Lemaire taps the puck to Frank Mahovlich bearing down on the left, and big Frank powders the puck into the left side of the cage, Cheevers diving frantically but a quarter-second too late.

Bucyk scores a minute later and the Bruins trail, 4–2, and now our attention focuses on Dryden. The frantic Bruins try to rev up their attack, storming in on the rookie, but he makes one incredible save after another. On a screen shot by Orr he loses sight of the puck. *Must be here,* he thinks, sticking up his glove, and the puck socks into it. *Luckiest save of my life.*

A little later Esposito drives right at him, drilling the puck from no more than 15 feet away, but up flies his glove and he snares the puck as it arrows toward the cage. He sees Espy slam his stick in frustration against the partition.

The time is blinking down to the final few seconds, the Bruins sitting on their bench, most with bowed heads, not wanting to watch what had been the unthinkable only three hours earlier. Then, the cup lost, they stand and skate out to shake the hands of the Canadiens. "Nice series," Espy says to Dryden.

The Candiens whooped into their clubhouse, where they bunched together, arms linked, and sang *Alouette*. All agreed that the Bruins looked flat, tired and maybe dispirited in the sixth and seventh games, their confidence shaken by Dryden's near-perfect goal-tending. Most pinpointed that second game, in which the Canadiens were losing 5–1, as the turning point. "That Richard goal when we were down 5–1 was the turning point," John Ferguson said. "It gave us the momentum."

Henri Richard revealed that the Canadiens had harassed Bobby Orr with their leftwinger. "That's right," Ferguson said. "Orr controlled the series up to the last two games," he told the *Herald Traveler's* Bill Kipouras. "I think it helped a great deal," Henri Richard added, "because Orr is 40 percent of their club and he looked tired. We checked him better these last two games."

The Bruins sat quietly in their clubhouse, most in their sweaty long johns, and when they did speak, their voices were only a soft mutter. Occasionally one grinned and made a wry joke. "Now I can make that date on April 24," Ken Hodge said, smiling, to a friend.

Bobby Orr came out of the showers and looked around. "I am going into hiding for the summer," he said.

"We blew it all in the second game with that 5–1 lead," Johnny McKenzie said, a cigarette dangling from his lips. "After that we never got back on the track."

Rick Smith sat hunched over a long bench. I approached him, notebook in hand. He looked up. "Please," he said, his eyes moist, "I don't want to talk about it."

I move over to Ken Hodge. "Well," he said, never finding it difficult to say what he thinks, "it took us 76 games to get here and seven games to lose here. But nothing can take away what we did this season—the records we set, all the games we won. I look upon the playoffs as a new season, and in that season we got beat."

"In a short series," Phil Esposito said, "a goaltender can get hot and beat you. But I don't mean that as any excuse.

They played better, they deserved it."

Someone asked Turk about his fight with John Ferguson near the end of the game. "Hell," Turk said in his curled-lip way, "it was the end of the season for us so I said to Ferguson, 'It's now or never,' and threw a punch at him."

I left the Bruin clubhouse slowly, reluctant to say goodbye to friends like Espy and Orr, friends made during this long season. As I walked down the Garden corridor I recalled that this was the 11th straight time the Canadiens had knocked the Bruins out of the Stanley Cup playoffs.

I suddenly remembered the name of the team that had beaten the Bruins in their first game way back in 1924. That team had been from Montreal.

Now it is months later, time for the playoffs to begin. Most of the previous season's Bruins are with the team with the exception of Wayne (Swoop) Carleton, who was sent to California. You already have met Bobby Orr and Phil Esposito. Now meet the rest of the Bruins on the eve of the 1971 —72 playoffs.

Chapter XIII

PIE, THE CHIEF, AND THE TERRIBLE ONE

Sitting in a Chicago motel room, Phil Esposito was ticking off the names of the players he thought the most popular on the Bruins. "Bobby Orr," he said, "is the most popular, and that's the way it should be because he is the best. And the fans love Derek Sanderson because of his long hair and the way he is always getting into fights. And they love Johnny McKenzie because of the way he rams up and down the ice knocking down people and digging out that puck. And that's also only right. Hell, if I were a fan I'd love Johnny McKenzie myself."

Opposing players do not love Johnny McKenzie. The 5-foot-9, 180-pound rightwinger—the Bruins call him "Pie" because of his round face—is a flesh-and-bone symbol of the Big Bad Bruins. He crashes into opponents with punishing forechecks as he rampages into the corners to dig out the puck. He dug out that puck so often during the 1970–71 season that his line—himself, Fred Stanfield and the veteran Johnny

(Chief) Bucyk—was the second-highest scoring line in the league, trailing only the record-shattering Esposito-Hodge-Cashman line. Johnny scored a career-high 31 goals, reaching the 30–goal mark that he had been trying to attain for the previous three seasons when he scored 29, 29 and 28.

The one goal he will never forget was scored in the fourth and final game of the Bruins' semi-final round against Chicago in the 1969–70 Stanley Cup series. With the score tied 4–4 late in the game, Johnny zoomed in on Black Hawk goalie Tony Esposito and whapped the puck into the nets to win the game.

"That was sweet, so sweet," Pie said later, "because that club, the Black Hawks, didn't have room for me a few years ago."

Not only the Black Hawks didn't have room for Pie. In 17 years of pro hockey—he broke in with Calgary way back in 1955—he has bounced from Chicago to Detroit to New York to Boston, with a lot of minor league way-stations in between. He came to the Bruins from the Rangers during the 1965–66 season and he was very happy to come to Boston. He'd been sitting on the bench in New York for half a season and figured he was on his way back to the minor leagues. He was accustomed to being shuttled around; he'd never stayed with any club for more than two seasons. But after five happy years in Boston, the 33-year-old Pie decided he'd be around a while longer, and he bought a house in nearby Lynnfield.

Actually, he is fortunate that he is playing hockey at all. In a game several years ago against the Toronto Maple Leafs, Pie tried to split the defense. A stick skewered Pie in the abdomen. He was carried off the ice and sped to a hospital, where surgeons operated to repair a ruptured spleen. Johnny came back to play hockey but it was a nasty affair. In his placid, smiling way Pie talks about the incident as though it had happened to someone else. But you sense immediately he know how close a call it was when he says:

"The doctors told me if they hadn't patched me up right away I'd have been dead in an hour or so."

Pie is accustomed to peril. For many years he rode bucking broncos and roped calves in rodeos like the Calgary Stampede. He was born in cowboy country, in High River, Alberta, on December 12, 1937, and until he moved to Lynnfield he spent his summers around High River as a cowpuncher.

There are some around the NHL who think that Pie does a little too much punching during the season. Certainly Pie has no love for someone in an opposing uniform. During Stanley Cup play it is customary for the players on each side to line up and shake hands after the final game.

Not Pie. He speeds off the ice. "Johnny doesn't hate anyone," a teammate once said, "but I don't think he'd shake hands with his own mother if she were on the other side."

Pie smiles when he hears something like that. "Look," he once told writer D. Leo Monahan. "If you don't throw the calf, he'll throw you."

That kind of toughness appeals to Boston Bruin fans, who like their heroes to be aggressive. After the 1969–70 season a Boston TV station conducted a poll for a Seventh Man Award, the idea being to salute a player the fans thought didn't get the credit he deserved. The winner was Pie.

Pie didn't let the award go to his head in the 1970–71 season. In addition to his 31 goals, he added 46 assists for 77 points, the sixth-highest point total on the team, and eighth best in the NHL. The fans tossed hats onto the ice on December 20 when he got his first hat-trick of the season, swatting home three goals against Minnesota. "Hey, Pie," Phil Esposito yelled at him that night in the clubhouse, "soon you're going to be getting more ink than Bobby."

Pie grinned. He didn't mind the attention after all those years of being ignored. "It's nice to play in Boston," he once said. "The fans appreciate me. They like a hitting game and my game is a hitting game."

Bruin general manager Milt Schmidt thought that Pie was hitting too many calves during the off-season at those rodeos. "You might get hurt and we need you, Pie," Schmidt told him. "I'd appreciate it if you would give up the calf-roping."

Pie agreed. And later he told a friend, "They had to be interested in me to show that kind of concern. It's certainly nice, after all those years, to feel wanted."

This was the night of January 24, 1971, in Boston Garden, applause swelling across the arena and descending on the bowed shoulders of the Bruin with the number "6" on his back. Surrounding No. 6 were some 30 gifts bestowed on him by fans, teammates, and even by the Bruins' opponents that night, the Montreal Canadiens. Number 6, Ted Green, stood at center ice, swallowing hard, unable to speak, and when Johnny Bucyk escorted his wife, Pat, to stand beside him, she broke into tears.

They were tears of happiness. For Ted Green had come back. Some 18 months earlier surgeons had picked bits of bone out of his brain and said they were reasonably sure he would live but they were not at all sure he would ever play another game of hockey. Ted's skull had been fractured in a stick fight with St. Louis' Wayne Maki. In a scuffle near the boards, Terrible Teddy had demonstrated how he won his nickname. "In the big games," he once said, "we try to beat the other guys up." In this game, he knocked down Maki.

Maki got up and thrust his stick at Green's abdomen. Green whirled and slammed his stick at Maki's head. Maki ducked, then cracked his stick across Green's right temple. Green dropped to the ice, his eyes glazed, his face contorted in a horrible grimace, blood splotching his hair and the ice.

He was given the last rites of the Catholic church. Then surgeons hovered over him for four hours, repairing the damaged skull. Later the doctors said they were concerned about his partially paralyzed left arm and numbed muscles on the left side of his face. He talked, one Bruin said, "like he had a broken jaw."

Surgeons operated twice on the skull. In the last operation they inserted a protective plate in his skull. It would protect the brain if he suffered another head injury, in a car accident, for instance. It seemed unlikely the skull would ever be injured in a hockey game; the brain injury had seemingly robbed Teddy of the quick reflexes one needs in the lightning-fast world of hockey. The reflexes were so poor, for instance, that Teddy—a five-handicap golfer before the injury—could shoot only a 110 the first time he played after the injury.

But Teddy said he would come back to hockey. In April, 1970, as his teammates were winning the Stanley Cup, he began to do calisthenics in the living room of his home in Winnipeg. He ran one to three miles a day to strengthen his legs. In July he moved from Winnipeg to Boston to work out daily at a gym. He played golf every day and one day came in with a 79. "That's when we knew Teddy had his coordination back," Bruin trainer Dan Canney told writer Edwin Kiester, Jr. "We heard he was really whaling the ball."

At the Bruin camp Teddy showed right away he was still the Terrible Teddy Green who had terrorized NHL forwards for nine years. In the Bruins' first scrimmage he hit a teammate with such force and ferocity that the flattened player's face turned white.

Still, the comeback was tortuous. In his first few games he was much too cautious with his passes. And he hesitated before he shot, missing openings at the cage. Someone asked him how far away he was from the All-Star defenseman he was in 1968. Teddy laughed, a hard laugh. "Ten miles," he said. "A hundred."

Later he told a friend, "I know I can play in the NHL again. What I don't know is how good I can play."

He proved he could play practically as well as ever. He totaled 42 points in the 1970–71 season, with five goals and 37 assists, and that was almost exactly what he had in each of the two previous seasons before he was hurt. His point total was the third highest among the Bruin defensemen. Early in the season he and Maki faced each other again. They looked into each other's eyes and nodded. The fight was in the past; Teddy Green was looking to the future.

He could hardly hold a grudge anyway, since if he held a grudge against every player he had ever tangled with, he wouldn't be speaking to half the players in the league. He'd piled into them all: Bobby Hull, Gordie Howe, Frank Mahovlich, John Ferguson—the big ones and the small ones. The toughest one in the league? "For my money," Teddy once said, "Gordie Howe is the toughest."

"Green always has been the unofficial team leader of the Bruins," ex-coach Harry Sinden once wrote. "He inspires players to be more courageous than they are. They simply don't want Teddy to think they don't want to mix it. They don't want him to say, 'That s.o.b. is chicken.' So they make sure they're not."

As long as he plays hockey, Teddy will have to wear a special form-fitted fiberglass helmet to protect him from another blow to the head. At first Teddy didn't like the helmet. "It seems to throw my equilibrium off or something," he said. But he grew accustomed to the helmet and again many people were asking why the NHL doesn't make it mandatory for all players to wear helmets—as football and baseball do. "It's foolish not to wear a helmet," Ted Green once said before his injury. "I don't because the other guys don't. I know that's silly but most of the players feel the same way. If the league made us do it, though, we'd all wear them and nobody would mind."

Certainly no one could ever question Ted's courage because he wore a helmet. In his first junior season, with the St.

Boniface Canadiens, he sat out ten of the team's 32 games under suspension for scrapping. Ted was born in St. Boniface on March 23, 1940, christened Edward Green, but now everyone calls him Ted or Teddy. He was signed by Montreal who lost him in the 1960 draft to Boston. "We just drafted a kid who could be another Eddie Shore," said then-general manager Lynn Patrick in one of those optimistic statements GMs are prone to make—especially when their team is losing.

Terrible Teddy Green never became another Eddie Shore except in one department: guts.

Johnny (Chief) Bucyk stared at Milt Schmidt across the general manager's desk. They had been talking in Schmidt's office on this day in the early fall of 1967. "Milt," Johnny Bucyk said, "I don't agree with you. I've been averaging close to 50 points a season. So how can you say I should be scoring more?"

"But look, Chief," Schmidt said. "Two-thirds of those points have been assists. We think you're too good a shooter to be passing when you should be shooting. We think you should be scoring more goals."

"I always work the corners and get the puck out," the chunky six-foot 215-pound leftwinger replied. "You can't score from the corners. If you pass off and the other guy scores, what's the difference? A goal is a goal."

Schmidt persisted. He wanted to offer Johnny an incentive to score more. He'd give the Chief a bonus for scoring so many goals.

Bucyk shook his head. "I don't want a bonus for goals. It would put too much pressure on me. Maybe if I had the opportunity to pass off I wouldn't and I'd take a shot I shouldn't take. Give me a bonus for total points."

Schmidt agreed. Near the end of that 1967–68 season Johnny spotted Schmidt at a practice session. "Hey, Milt," he yelled. "aren't you glad I don't have a bonus clause for goals?"

Milt grinned. Indeed he had reason to be happy. Johnny would have won that bonus money for he had blasted 30 shots into the nets for goals. But Johnny had won the bonus money for total points. With 39 assists to go with those 30 goals, he had scored 69 points—a career high.

After that season you didn't hear people around the Garden saying that the Chief should be scoring more goals. In 1970–71 he whapped 51 pucks into the nets, second only to Phil Esposito on the club. Working on a line with Fred Stanfield and John McKenzie, he collected 65 assists, more than anyone on the club except Esposito and Orr, for a total of 116 points, also third behind Espy and Bobby.

He was on the road to setting a slew of Bruins' all-time records. At 35, he has played in more games than any other Bruin in the team's history, he has collected more assists than any other Bruin and he has scored more points than any other Bruin.

The Chief will never forget the night of December 8, 1967, when he rifled a puck past Ranger goalie Ed Giacomin for his 576th point as a Bruin, breaking the record that had been set by Milt Schmidt.

The huge crowd in the Boston Garden began to chant, "Chief . . . Chief . . . Chief . . . " The crowd continued to chant even as play resumed. "That applause, it does something to you," the Chief said later. "First you think you're dreaming. Then it hits you. They're cheering for you. It hits hard. But it's wonderful. Now people stop me in the street and say hello. Before they'd look but they wouldn't say hello. I like to say hello to people. It makes me feel good."

He has reason to feel good because his climb to fame was not an easy one for the Chief (he got the name because he resembles an Indian but actually he is of Ukranian ancestry). The Chief was born in Edmonton, Alberta, on May 12, 1935.

His father died when he was ten and his mother was in poor health. Johnny left school after the 11th grade to work as a mechanic for a Ford dealer, on whose hockey team he was playing.

At 16 he was a brawny six-foot 200-pounder. Being so big, he was an ungainly skater. His coach sent him to a figure-skating school. There big John whirled through pirouettes and figure-8's with the girls and hoped, sneaking out of the place, that none of his friends would see him.

His skating improved and in 1954, at 18, he signed to play pro hockey with the Edmonton Flyers of the Western Hockey League. That season he skated on a line with Bronco Horvath at center and Vic Stasiuk on the right wing, a line that later became famous in Boston as the Uke line, because all three were of Ukranian descent.

He came to Boston by way of Detroit, which brought him up after he was named Rookie of the Year in the WHL. "I never thought I'd make the NHL," Johnny says now. "Then, boom, I'm with the Wings. Gordie Howe and Ted Lindsay. I'd always idolized them."

He played only intermittently for Detroit during his two seasons with the Wings. He came to Boston in 1957 for the late goalie Terry Sawchuk.

The Bruins were winners during his first two seasons with the team, going to the finals of the Stanley Cup playoffs both years before bowing to Montreal. Then came the losing years, the team no better than fifth. In those years, although Johnny averaged close to 50 points a season, he heard booing from the Garden fans and grumbling from the front office.

Suddenly he started to score more goals. What had happened? Harry Sinden had one theory. "He's an easy, unassuming guy," Sinden said. "It was tough for him to get excited before each game. Now he is approaching each game with a more concentrated attitude. Especially now that we have a winning team. Each game has meaning. There's

Orr soars through air after scoring goal that won the Stanley Cup.

something at stake. It's bringing out his full potential, and the guy's loaded with talent."

Bucyk himself thought the fans had helped. "In the past, when they were on me, I'd push and press a lot and I wouldn't produce as much. It was good to have them with me."

The Chief also concedes that now he is more tense and "up" for games. "I get awful nervous," he says, "which means I'm getting worked up and a little excited. I cough and gag and choke. Then one of the guys will come over and ask me how I'm feeling. 'Lousy,' I'll say. 'Good,' they'll say. 'That means you're going to have a good game.' And they go away laughing."

But it was true: he did play better when he was coughing and gagging and choking. He was coughing and gagging and choking something terrible on December 10, 1970, as he got ready to play his 1,000th NHL game. That night he figured in the scoring of six goals. On January 3, 1971, he coughed and choked and gagged and went out and scored three goals against Vancouver. On March 4 he coughed and choked and gagged and got his third hat-trick of the season against the Seals.

Cough and choke and gag. That's the Chief before a game. During a game he's plain good hockey.

Chapter XIV

THE SWINGING TURK

"I know I'm colorful," The Turk was saying. He was talking to a writer, Les Bridges. The Turk lit a cigarette and leaned back. "Orr," he said, "has got the overall talent. Esposito has got the overall points. The field left for me is color."

Derek (The Turk) Sanderson is colorful by being many things to many people. Many exciting things: the on-ice brawler, the off-ice lover, the bearded hippie thumbing his nose at the Establishment, the witty TV talk show host, the humorous writer of a book, *I Have to Be Me,* the eccentric individualist who just might drop hockey and go off to live in Europe "with the grooviest chick I can find."

"The thing to remember about Derek," his attorney Bob Woolf once told writer Bill Bruns, "is that he's always looking for ways to shock people. His whole life is built that way. He's dying to be important."

There are some in the NHL who think that The Turk just might die trying to be important. After Teddy Green's head injury Derek became the "cop," the chief head-hunter, the brawler, the villain of the Bruins. Once he explained his philosophy—and, by extension, the Bruins' philosophy—in dealing with the opposition. "I feel it is important to draw first blood. I like to get hit early so I can hit back. That gets me up. Then when my teammates see this, they take offense and they join in and then everybody is loose."

He pleaded guilty to one charge often made against him. "Sure I'm a dirty player," he said, a glint in his eyes. "I like playing dirty. Anyway that's the way the game should be played. I like fighting. So what if I lose a couple of teeth? I'm going to lose them anyway, sooner or later. It doesn't bother me. It's only pain. It doesn't hurt for long."

"Sanderson is an agitator," Ranger goalie Ed Giacomin says. "He says things to get you mad. Like 'we're going to put that puck right between your eyes tonight.'"

In the 1970 Stanley Cup series against the Bruins, the Rangers tried to use those needling tactics against Sanderson. Just before a faceoff Giacomin left his goal position and skated out to the faceoff circle. He looked at Derek and said, something like, "Keep your head up, we're gonna get you."

Derek, never one to underestimate himself, assumed New York coach Emile Francis had put a price on his head: the Rangers were out to get him. "That's cool, groovy," Derek snapped back at Giacomin. "Take your best shot."

He turned to other Rangers. "Any of you other beeping guys want to do it, take your best shot."

Moments later the referee dropped the puck for the faceoff. As he nearly always does, Derek won the faceoff. He flipped the puck into the corner. He went after it and caught an elbow from Ranger Dave Balon.

Derek flashed an elbow and knocked down Balon. A second Ranger veered in on him, Derek tossed off his gloves and threw a looping right that staggered the Ranger. A third Ranger leaped on top of Turk, and all three fell to the ice in a writhing heap.

"I was throwing punches when I didn't even know who I was throwing them at," the Turk said later. "Anybody in a dark blue shirt I was swinging for . . . I got out of that brawl finally and there was another going on along the boards so I got into that one. When it broke up, there was (Ranger) Bill Fairbairn trying to play the role, mouthing off. A linesman was between us saying, 'Forget him, forget him, don't get into trouble.' Linesmen are always trying to convince you of that. Trying to calm you down." Derek laughed.

"I was trying to jockey into a different position so I could sucker Fairbairn. Finally I made a left turn and the linesman made a right turn so I charged Fairbairn and we ended up in a fight. Then the referee went and made a bad call. He threw me out of the game." Balon also was ousted.

An angry Derek charged that Emile Francis deliberately had schemed to get him out of the game. Francis laughed when someone told him what the Turk had said, "Why," asked Francis, "would we trade a 33-goal player like Balon for an 18-goal player like Sanderson? I went to school. I can subtract."

But later Francis admitted that goals alone did not tell how much the Turk meant to the Bruins. "He is a helluva hockey player," Francis said. "He kills penalties for the Bruins and he kills you in the process because how are you gonna beat a team that won't let you score on them when you got them down by a man? He is one of the best on faceoffs and he's got a mean steak in him which is nice to have in hockey. I'll tell you who he reminds me of—he reminds me of Eddie Stanky."

Eddie Stanky was a second-baseman with the Dodgers, Giants and Braves of whom it once was said, "He can't hit, he can't field, he can't throw. He just beats you with the intangibles."

The Turk's leading intangible is his menacing, muscular

body that body-checks opponents with bruising ferocity, wilting their aggressiveness. "If you don't hit them around the nets early," the Turk says, "they'll come flying in there. If you hit them, they aren't so eager."

He is amused, though, by the lack of size he brings to his job. He is six-foot and 168 pounds. At times during the season his weight slips to 163. "There are guys in this league who could beat me up," he says with a devilish grin. "But it hasn't happened yet in over two-dozen fights."

The Turk contributes more than muscles, but again they are things only the experts notice. For example, it was a perfect pass by Sanderson onto Bobby Orr's stick that set up the tie-breaking goal by Orr in the final game of the 1969–70 Stanley Cup playoffs, the goal that brought the Cup back to Boston after 29 years of waiting.

At the start of the next season, 1970–71, The Turk said he had adopted a new image: no longer would he be a brawler on the ice. That image didn't last long: by midseason he was checking and punching as indiscriminately as usual. "I hate to lose," he growled. "I hate to lose whether it's playing gin or shooting pool. Losers, they date college girls. The winners date Playboy bunnies. That's why I hate those guys out on the ice who are in different uniforms. They're out there to make me a loser. I hate 'em, really hate 'em." Derek wanted to title his autobiography, *I'll Smash You in the Face*.

His pugnacity has helped to hide his other assets. In the 1970–71 record-breaking Bruin season, he rapped in 29 goals and had 34 assists for a total of 63 points. Only Esposito scored more goals among the Bruin centermen.

"He's got a couple of things going for him that you can't teach," Milt Schmidt says. "He has anticipation and balance. He is always around the puck and it takes a tank to knock him down.

"He's also one of the top penalty killers in the league. Sanderson is the kind of player you put on the ice late in the game when you're either one goal ahead or one goal behind. He can help you at both ends of the rink. He's probably the best sweep checker in the NHL."

To sweep check, a player drops onto one knee to sweep or kick the puck away from the opponent. Of course it exposes a man's face to a 100-mph. whizzing puck, but doctors have been sewing stitches in Derek's face ever since he was a kid back in Niagara Falls. (His father, in fact, collected a jar of those stitches taken from Derek's face and body during his Junior hockey days.)

Old-timers in hockey admire Derek's poke-checking, an art little practiced by most players today. "Watch him poke-check," Schmidt says. "The end of his stick goes back and forth like a snake's tongue."

Even opponents who detest Sanderson concede he is probably the best centerman in the league on faceoffs. It annoys Derek that so few fans appreciate his skill at capturing the puck when sticks collide in the faceoff circle. "People think the faceoff is nothing, just chopped liver," Derek says, frowning. "You just drop the puck and that's it. Who cares? But if it's dropped and you win it—and you win all of them all night, then you have possession of the puck and the other guys have to take it away from you. Consequently you control the game."

In one 1969–70 Stanley Cup playoff game against the Black Hawks, Derek entered 15 faceoff duels. He won 14 and the Bruins were 6–3 victors.

"Gerry Cheevers knows I can win faceoffs," Derek says. "That's why he will hold the puck so often when he stops a shot, rather than throwing it into the corner where someone else can take another shot at goal."

All the 1970–71 Bruins appreciated the intangibles that Derek contributed to their record-breaking season. What some resented, though, was Derek's casual attitude toward practice sessions. The day before the seventh and final game against the Canadiens in the 1971 playoffs, Tom Johnson called a light practice. The Turk did not appear and there was talk that Johnson fined him. One Bruin grumbled: "This is the biggest game we've had all season and he can't give up a few hours to get ready for it."

Derek smiles sheepishly when he hears such reproofs. "You know," he was saying one day, "Johnny Bucyk has been late for practice just twice in 13 years. I was late 13 times in one month.

"The team knows I don't care about money. They tell me it's going to cost me five hundred dollars. I say that's cool. Don't give me a lecture. Just take the money. Like I missed a curfew in Philadelphia and they fined me. I missed a curfew in New York and they fined me. We were on a three-day trip and I got fined three times for missing curfew. I don't hassle these things. If I'm wrong, fine me. If I'm right, I'll stick up for my rights."

At the start of the 1970–71 season Derek stuck up for his rights about the salary he was being paid by the Bruins. The Bruins had signed him to a three-year contract at $13,000 a year when he first came into the league in 1967–68. "I was rookie of the year that season," Sanderson said. "I asked them for a raise. But they wouldn't give me one. I told them I was going to hold out. But they said I couldn't because I was under contract.

"I would have held out anyway. But I didn't because I don't play hockey for the Bruins. I don't play for them or the league or myself. I play for the other seventeen guys on the team."

He was still being paid $13,000 a year, Derek said, even after helping the team win the Stanley Cup. That news made black headlines in Boston. Bruin board chairman Weston W. Adams exploded. "It is not our style to reveal salaries," Adams said. "We feel it is a private affair. But the present situation, which is ridiculous, forces it on us."

The Turk's salary, Adams said, included $14,000 from his base salary, a $12,000 bonus from the team, $3,000 in insurance payments, plus another $10,000 from the league in bonus payments for finishing second and winning the Stanley Cup.

Some newspapermen, siding with Derek, pointed out that his payments from the Bruins were well below the $40,000 and $50,000 salaries paid to sixth and seventh men on pro basketball teams like the Celtics, who have never drawn as well as the Bruins.

"In all fairness to the hockey teams," said attorney Bob Woolf, who was trying to get more money for Derek, "the National Hockey League doesn't have the big television contract." Thus while each pro football team gets $1.54 million per season from the networks, a hockey team like the Bruins receives only $100,000 a season from its one-game-a-week contract with the networks.

"The big difference in hockey salaries," said Woolf, "is the money that goes to the star, the superstar and the rookie. In hockey the stars and the superstars don't get the high salaries that they get in other sports. The average player in hockey, however, probably gets as much as the average player in any other sport."

For the 1971–72 season the Turk talked loudly about a contract for at least $60,000 plus bonuses. And if he didn't get it, he said, he would quit. "I am mentally prepared to quit," he told a friend. "Besides it wouldn't be so hard because I hate to fly. I'm not afraid of getting banged up on ice. But flying is something else. When something happens on a plane, it's all over. Finalized. No more girls, no nothing. I don't dig that."

Derek Sanderson was born in Niagara Falls, Ontario, on June 16, 1946. He grew up in a dead-end neighborhood where a pair of quick fists helped to keep a kid healthy. Derek

carried the brawling onto the ice. If you are to believe him—
there is a bit of the story-teller in him at times —he had 46
on-ice battles during his two years of junior hockey for the
Niagara Falls Flyers.

In 1965 and 1966 he made brief appearances with the
Bruins while playing six games during those two seasons with
the Bruins' Oklahoma City farm team. He reported to the
Bruins' training camp at London in the fall of 1967.

"They put me on what must have been the seventh line,"
he remembers, "and I figured I'd be on the next plane to
Oklahoma City. But Phil Esposito told me I'd stick and he
was right. I thought I should stick but I didn't know whether
the Bruin management had the brains to recognize my
talent."

Espy also predicted that Derek would be the rookie of the
year. True enough, after Derek scored 24 goals and earned
25 assists that 1967–68 season, he won the Calder Trophy as
the league's outstanding rookie.

He had come to that first Bruin camp in a wash-and-wear
suit. The rookie of the year came to camp the second year in
mod suits and bell bottoms. "Reporters would ask me how
many suits I owned," Derek once told Bill Bruns. "I'd say
47 suits and 69 pairs of shoes and boots. Actually I had only
two pairs of shoes and a couple of suits. But I lied so often I
began to believe it."

The dead-end kid was trying to adopt a new style of living,
a swinging style adopted by his two idols and pals—Ken
Harrelson, then the mod slugger for the Red Sox, and Joe
Namath, the playboy-quarterback of the football world.
Derek's sideburns grew longer, he sported a Namath-style
Fu-Manchu mustache, and if Namath came to Boston with
two beauties on each arm, the Turk had to be seen with three
beauties on each arm.

Like Namath, he rented a fancy apartment with heavy
bearskin rugs on the floor and garish decorations. And like

Namath, he heard the jeering crowd. He made insulting gestures at booing fans and once climbed out of a penalty box in Philadelphia to swing at a pair of fans. Often he had to dodge barrages of hot coffee, beer, metal coins and even padlocks thrown at him in out-of-town arenas by fans angered by his beard, long hair and contemptuous manner. "I go better when I'm booed," he says, "And anyway anything is OK as long as people notice you."

Like Namath and Harrelson, he is fiercely outspoken and rebellious toward authority. He has been the host on a weekly TV talk show in Boston and has also appeared on the Johnny Carson and Merv Griffin national TV shows. On the shows he talked witheringly of NHL brass, in particular his special antagonist, league president Clarence Campbell. But in his loose way Derek never got too serious. Once, on his show, he said, "I'm a firm believer that to be sane you have to be insane."

Off the camera he could be much more serious. Once, in the Bruin dressing room after a game, he called Campbell a stuffed shirt. Tom Johnson overheard and snapped, "Why don't you keep your mouth shut and quit looking for the headlines?"

"I was just telling the truth and you know it."

"We've had enough of your popping off," Johnson growled. "He's still a bum."

Johnson strode angrily away. "See, Derek," veteran Eddie Westfall said. "Like I've been telling you since training camp—you pop off and then you have to pull yourself out of the hole."

"I have got to say what I believe."

"I know," Westfall said. "But not when the press is around. You only hurt yourself."

Derek stared for a moment at the floor. "It takes maturity and self-control, Eddie," he said, "and I don't have that yet."

When he gets that maturity—if he does—Derek Sanderson may be a better hockey player. But he may not be nearly as much fun.

Chapter XV

A TEAM OF MANY THREADS

Bobby Orr once called the 1970–71 Bruins "a team of brothers." There are the superstars on this team, of course: the faces of Orr and Esposito and Sanderson are well known to the public. But the team gets its character and personality from the character and personality of each of its members, threaded together in a tight ball, and without knowing what these other men are like, you cannot know the team.

You start with No. 1, Eddie Johnston, the 36-year-old goalie, a Bruin since the 1962–63 season. You see his bulky 6-foot-1 body standing like a boulder in front of the cage, the face blanked by his mask, and you remember that he is the fourth-oldest Bruin in service; only Bucyk, Westfall and Greenie have been around longer. You also might recall that he is the team's player representative.

But you might not know that he wouldn't miss a big golf tournament in the east if he can help it (a native of Montreal, he now lives in Stoneham, Mass.). He himself bangs the little white ball around a course in the 70s, and some of the Bruins will tell you that Ed could make a dollar or two following the pro trail. Sanderson's golf game also has promise.

A Bruin rubs his chin reflectively as he talks about Johnston. "Cheevers got hurt late in the 1969–70 season when we were in the middle of a tough race. Ed stepped right in and gave us back-to-back shutouts against Montreal and Chicago. Then, in the playoffs, he was back sitting on the bench. He has played in only a couple of playoff games in the past three seasons, even though last season he played almost as many minutes as Cheesy did during the regular season. If anybody has a right to complain it is Ed, but he doesn't because all that matters is that the team wins."

Ed was born on November 25, 1935, growing up in Montreal, where he played for the Junior Canadiens. He broke in as a pro for Winnipeg in the 1956–57 season. He came to Boston in 1962 when the team was at the bottom, and in those early years he got little help from his defensemen. He has split the job in recent years with Gerry Cheevers, and maintained a respectable average of around three-goals-against per game. A quiet-spoken, taciturn, even-tempered man, Ed grins when someone says the Bruins win with their offense, not with their defense. "The only thing that's important," he says, "is that we win."

Mike (Shaky) Walton came to Boston midway through the 1970–71 season in search of a victory within himself. He had been playing for the Toronto Maple Leafs and he had been unhappy with his own play and the way the Leafs were using him. He was so unhappy he was treated by doctors for depression. Finally, the doctors suggested that Shaky, as the players were calling him, be traded. When Shaky came into the Bruin dressing room for the first time, he saw Bobby Orr, his pal and co-owner of a hockey school. "Hey, Shaky," Bobby said with a grin, "did you bring your psychiatrist's couch with you?"

Mike grinned and said, "No, I carry a portable one with me."

Everyone laughed and Shaky Walton, just like that, was a Bruin. A few weeks later Derek Sanderson was injured. Mike Walton took his place and centered the line, himself popping in six goals while helping on 21 others for a grand total of 27 points, surprisingly high considering he played only about half the season.

Mike was born in Kirkland Lake, Ontario, on January 3, 1945. He played junior hockey with the Toronto Marlboros and after five years in the minors he joined the Maple Leafs for the 1966–67 season. Up until 1970–71 and his medical problem, he'd been a consistent 20-goal man, a 5-foot-9, 170-pound whizbang who has a wicked lefthanded shot. "We're happy to have Mike," says coach Tom Johnson. "Getting him could be one of our better moves."

Perhaps the most talkative of all the Bruins—he can go word for word against Turk—is Ken Hodge, the 27-year-old right-winger who is the brawniest of the big bad Bruins: 6–foot–2 and 215 pounds. It is Ken's job, along with Wayne Cashman, to dig the puck out of the corners and pass to it Espy—hockey's greatest scorer.

Ken says he doesn't mind doing all that punishing work for Espy. "I get paid for assists as well as goals," he says, "they count the same. And I can go to the cage after he shoots and pick up his garbage."

He got his share of goals in 1970–71—43—along with 62 assists for 105 points. He, Espy and Cash scored more points in one season than any hockey line in history—336. And Ken's name is also in the record books for having piled up more points in one season than any rightwinger in NHL history.

Ken was born in Birmingham, England, on June 25, 1944.

He grew up in St. Catharine's, Ontario, where he played junior hockey. He played three seasons at Chicago before coming to Boston with Espy and Fred Stanfield. Now he lives in Lynnfield with his wife, Mary, their two children, with whom he splashes in a swimming pool shaped like a figure 8—his Bruin number.

On the leftwing of that high-scoring Esposito line is willowy Wayne Cashman, and playing on the left side wouldn't seem easy for Cash, as the Bruins call him, since he is a right-handed shot. But Cash doesn't mind: the climb to big-league stardom was a slow one for him. He was hobbled by injuries and spent several years bobbing up and down between Boston and the minor leagues. When Ron Murphy retired, the Bruins tried a number of hopefuls at leftwing, and all were found wanting. So Cash was thrust into the spot, righty or not. He got off the shots with zero-zero accuracy and last season he popped in 21 goals, the first time he topped the 20-mark in his career. His forte, though, is passing off the puck to the scorers, and of all the 1970–71 Bruins only Orr, Esposito, Bucyk and Hodge had more assists.

The blond, curly-haired Cash was born in Kingston, Ontario, on June 24, 1945, and played with Bobby Orr on the Oshawa Generals. The first pro hockey game he ever played, in 1964–65, was as a big leaguer, in a Bruin uniform, and he has been with the Bruins every year since, although he did time for three seasons in the minors. Off season he lives in Verona, Ontario, with his wife and two children.

Perhaps the most underrated player in the league is 27-year-old Fred Stanfield, the "quiet man" center of the Bruins who doesn't score as many goals as fellow-center Esposito nor talk as loudly as centerman Derek Sanderson. But in 1970–71 Fred's line—himself, Bucyk, and McKenzie—accounted for 106 goals and 269 points, the second-highest scoring line, behind Espy's, in the league.

Fred himself finished with 24 goals and 52 assists, which tied him for ninth place in points with a pretty fair center: Jean Beliveau.

"Deep and silent, that pretty well sums up Fred Stanfield," Derek Sanderson says, somewhat incredulous that anyone could be so quiet. "He's deeply and silently proud to be where he is. And don't ever make a bet with him and not pay off. He'll hound you."

A clever passer in the classic mode of a centerman, Fred also snaps off whizzing low shots on goal. But he will never be a high scorer on a team with shooters like Espy and Orr. He contributes to those scores, though, by wearing down opponents. He is 5–10 and 186 pounds and hits hard. "A great hitter, a solid bodychecker," Turk says. "Fred is easily one of the best-hitting forwards in the league. But he does his checking cleanly, and therefore his toughness almost goes unnoticed."

Born in Toronto on May 4, 1944, Fred played his amateur hockey with the St. Catharines TeePees. He joined Chicago in 1964–65 without any minor-league hockey, but he wasn't big and rough enough for coach Billy Reay and Fred spent most of his time killing penalties. And he was unhappy with the little money he was getting. He was very happy to come to last-place Boston with Esposito and Hodge. "I knew I'd get to play with Boston," he says with a grin.

Now he lives in St. Catharines, not far from Gerry Cheevers. "He bought a house down the street from mine," says the mischievous Cheesy, "but his is a lot cheaper than mine."

The 30-year-old Cheesy, the team's No. 1 goaltender, is a kind of Don Rickles in the Bruin dressing room, along with Esposito and Sanderson. They needle most everyone. And on the road Cheesy can be at his comic best hovering over a billiard table, cigarette dangling from his lips, tossing out wisecracks and insults as he pops ball after ball into the pockets.

The blocky, 5-foot-11, 195-pound Cheevers was born December 2, 1940, in St. Catharines and played junior hockey at St. Michaels College. He fended off shots in the Toronto chain for three years. Boston obtained him in the 1965–66 draft. He prepped for two more seasons at Oklahoma City and then took over as the Bruins' No. 1 net-minder in 1967–68. In the 1969–70 Stanley Cup triumph, Cheesy yielded an average of only two goals a game during a ten-game winning streak by Boston that brought the Cup back to New England.

With some of that Stanley Cup money, Cheesy bought a Thoroughbred, Cenacle's Image, and started his Four Thirty Stable, four for Bobby Orr's number and 30 for his. Cheesy hopes to win back some of the money he has deposited at race tracks over the years. Ever since he was a boy, "hot-walking" mounts at a track, he has liked the racing scene. "I have my savings," he says, "but I blow my money easily."

Cheesy is thankful for the relatively new face mask in hockey. "To me," he says, "the mask is the greatest invention since sliced bread. Without the mask I'd be a coward out there."

One Bruin who hasn't the time to be cowardly is Eddie Westfall, the 30-year-old handyman of the Bruins who has played every position except goaltender since he came to Boston in 1962–63. His most demanding job is shadowing the other team's big scorer. In the 1969–70 Stanley Cup playoff against Chicago, Eddie was glued so close to Bobby Hull that the blond superstar could take only a half-dozen shots on goal in three games.

"The thing about Eddie," says Milt Schmidt, "is that he has the knack of covering the big scorers like Hull without throwing his arms around them. Eddie plays squarely and fairly, he doesn't hook and hold like some of those other shadow-men."

Up until 1970–71 Eddie had never scored more than 18 goals. But in that record-shattering season he whipped 25 pucks into the nets and had 34 assists for 59 points. He is now an accomplished forward after starting out in his career as a defenseman.

Vernon Edward Westfall was born in Belleville, Ontario, on September 19, 1940, and played junior hockey for the Niagara Falls Flyers, while a tyke named Derek Sanderson watched from the seats. Eddie joined the Bruins in 1962–63 and hasn't allowed his varied duties on defense and offense to stop him from scoring; in his career he has smacked home 108 goals and collected 187 assists for 295 points. In the off-seasons he comes down to Boston from his home in Pelham, N.H., to make after-dinner speeches with poise and good-humor. And though some of the other Bruins might debate this, he is generally considered to be the team's best-dressed man.

Another versatile performer is young leftwinger Don Mar-cotte, only 24 years old at the end of the 1970–71 season. A quiet, even-voiced French Canadian, he usually sits in a cor-ner during the Bruins' team parties. As is so often the case, his wife is exactly the opposite—the bouncy life of the party.

Don has been a spare-time performer and does his job well and without complaint. "His value," says Milt Schmidt, "is that he can sit on a bench for a period and then come out and take a regular shift without looking stiff and uncertain. It's hard to do. Some guys would use that situation as a crutch, saying 'how can you expect me to do well when I can't get the feel of the game on the bench?' They'd be right, too. And Don has a right to complain. But he doesn't, and you won't find many who are like Don."

Don's other value is his ability to play left or right wing

equally well. Often he is on the ice to kill penalties. Don killed penalties so well in 1970–71 that he helped set one of the many Bruin scoring records. The Bruins scored more goals while shorthanded in one season than any other team in history: a whopping total of 25. Of those 25, Don slammed in five.

The wavy-haired Don was born in Arthabaska, Quebec, on April 15, 1947, and played amateur hockey for the Niagara Falls Flyers. After four years of learning he came up to the Bruins in 1968–69 and quickly impressed the Bruins with the solid weight of his checking. "Don," says one Bruin, "just may be the heaviest checker on the team."

Another quiet Bruin who saves his energy for smacking down people on the ice is big defenseman Don Awrey. "Don doesn't say much in the clubhouse," Milt Schmidt says. "But he goes out and does the job. And for whatever reason, he plays better in the playoffs. Don really helped us to win the Stanley Cup with five big assists. He'd had only ten assists all season long."

Now 28 years old, Don was playing with the Bruins way back in the 1963–64 season. He's been with the team ever since, except for occasional trips to the minors.

Don has never really left Kitchener, Ontario, however, where he was born on July 18, 1943, and still lives. After junior hockey with the Niagara Falls Flyers, he jumped immediately to Boston in 1963–64 to play 16 games before being shipped down for more experience. His best season was 1970–71 when he slapped in four goals and set up teammates for 21 assists—a 25-point total that was almost double his point total of any previous season.

Unlike Don, "Ace" Bailey lets you know that he is around. The swinging Bruin leftwinger is an up-and-coming Derek Sanderson, *sans* mustache. "On and off the ice," Milt

Schmidt says, "Ace is very aggressive and I won't say any more than that." Schmidt smiles. The Ace is a bachelor who gets around, a husky blond guy who looks like a southern California surfer.

"The Ace likes his fun," says Tom Johnson, "but once a game starts he is all business. He is the good holler man on the bench that every team needs. And he is the rugged kind who can battle his way out of the corners to get to the net for a good close shot."

Garnet E. Bailey, the Ace's real name, was born in Lloydminster, Saskatchewan, on June 13, 1948, and still makes his home there during the off-season. After playing amateur hockey with the Edmonton Oil Kings, he was lifted out of the Detroit farm system by the Bruins in the 17-year-old draft in 1967. After two years in the minors he joined the Bruins for the 1968–69 season. Late in the 1969–70 season he broke an ankle, missed the Stanley Cup playoffs, and has been slowly but resolutely coming back from that injury.

Two Bruins who are listeners rather than talkers are the Smith boys—Dallas and Rick Smith (they are not related except in temperament). Even in a winning clubhouse they say little and when the Bruins lose they usually go off and gloom over the defeat in solitude.

Dallas Smith teams up on defense with Bobby Orr, so it is no surprise that he gets very little publicity. But Milt Schmidt tells you what the Bruins think of Dallas: "He is the most underrated defenseman in the National Hockey League."

Bobby Orr agrees. "Dallas," he says, "does it all on defense. I can take chances rushing with the puck over the blue line into the opposition's ice because I know we got Dallas back there on defense."

Dallas was born October 10, 1941, in Hamiota, Manitoba, and played junior hockey with the Estevan, Saskatchewan,

Bruins. He came to the big-league Bruins only 18 years old at the start of the 1959–60 season, then bounced around the minors, learning the crafty ways of a defenseman, for almost six years. He came back to the Bruins to stick in 1967–68. His best season was 1970–71 when he flicked seven goals into the nets and assisted on 38 others for 45 points. He will always skate in the shadow of Bobby Orr but Dallas Smith, says Milt Schmidt, "has a great future in the NHL."

Dallas is a farmer in the off-season, he and his wife and two children going off to the seclusion of their home near Crandall in Manitoba.

His namesake, Rick Smith, doesn't appear to be the quiet type. With a crooked grin spreading down his face, he looks as though born—like Scaramouche—"with the gift of laughter and the sense that the world was mad." Yet he is as quiet as Dallas Smith. A bachelor, he isn't fond of the swinging places where you will find Turk Sanderson or Ace Bailey. You're more likely to find Rick reading a book for his pre-med course at Queens University; he hopes to be a dentist when he finishes his NHL career.

A heavyweight 5–foot–11 and 198 pounds, Rick is the bulwark that coaches like to see around the cage. And he can get the clutch points. In that final Stanley Cup game against St. Louis in 1970, the game that Orr won with a goal in overtime, it was Rick who popped in Boston's first goal and then assisted on the tying goal that sent the game into overtime. In the 1970–71 season he scored four goals and had 19 assists for 23 points—the highest in his three-year NHL career.

The banana-nosed Rick (his real name is Richard) was born on June 29, 1948, in Hamilton, Ontario. He played junior hockey for the Hamilton Red Wings, then played briefly on the Bruin farm at Oklahoma City in 1968–69 before coming to Boston that same season. Bruin coach Tom Johnson, ex-defenseman, says that all Rick needs to be among the best in the league is experience.

The coach of the team, big Tomcat, as he was known in his playing days, is more like a big brother—he is 41—than a paternal figure to the Bruins. Tom Johnson goes to sleep wearing a bow-tie, or so it is alleged, since he is never seen in public without one. Except, of course, when he was playing defense for 13 years with the Montreal Canadiens. In 1959 he won the Norris Trophy as the NHL's outstanding defenseman. "That was the year Doug Harvey was injured," he once said, but his modesty could not explain away his entry in 1970 into hockey's Hall of Fame.

He finished out his career with the Bruins and then was Harry Sinden's assistant, replacing Harry in 1970. After his appointment as head coach, Tom was asked: "Tom, did you ever coach anywhere before this?"

"No," Tom replied, "but I spent 23 years second-guessing guys who did."

In Tom's first year as coach the Bruins were first in the NHL East. After the season, despite the disappointing loss in the playoffs to the Canadiens, the Bruins showed what they thought of Tom by signing him to a new contract with a raise in pay. In the off-season Tom lives in West Concord on the outer edge of Boston.

The Bruins. The Big Bad Bruins. In this 1971-72 season the questions persist: How good are these Big Bad Bruins? Was the winning of the cup in 1970 a fluke? Was the failure of the team in the 1971 Stanley Cup playoffs a telltale sign of the team's lack of greatness? Or, on the other hand, was the winning of first place and the failure in the playoffs only a replay of what happened to the great team of 1938–41? That team won the cup in 1939, finished first but failed to win it in 1940, then came back to win it again in 1941.

Can the Bruins come back in 1971–72 to win the cup again? We take our questions to the man who is probably the greatest of all Bruins—past or present. We go to find Bobby Orr.

Chapter XVI

BOBBY ORR LOOKS AHEAD
"WHAT THE BRUINS MUST DO TO COME BACK"

He yawned, perched on the edge of the bed. It was a little after nine o'clock in the morning here at the Bay Shore Inn, the warm morning sunlight flashing through the windows. From outside you could dimly hear the bustle of the traffic as Vancouver roused itself for another day. Bobby Orr had come here for a business conference with his lawyer, Alan Eagleson, and to speak at a banquet this evening, one of dozens he'd attended this spring and summer, honoring him for what he is—the best all-around player in hockey today—and for what he may one day be—the greatest all-around player in the history of the game.

Some three months had passed by since that Sunday afternoon in Boston when the Canadiens had beaten the Bruins in the seventh game of the Stanley Cup playoffs. They had been relaxing but not especially merry months for Bobby. He'd stayed around Boston for a short time, then spent a month in

Florida, flopped out on sandy beaches and letting the hot sun restore the energy sapped by the long season. Every once in a while, the memory of that defeat sneaked up on him and stung the heart. In the clubhouse after the seventh game he had stayed in the showers a long time. When he came out he walked by his buddy, assistant trainer John "Frosty" Forristal, and muttered, "Well, I guess I got to talk to them sometime." He had talked to the press and made small jokes to hide his anger. But there was no way to bury the inner rage he felt, even now, months after the defeat. "It hurt Bobby deeply," Alan Eagleson told me a few days before my talk with Bobby in Vancouver. "He still feels it very badly."

On this sunny morning, though, as he talked in the hotel room here in Vancouver, none of the disappointment showed on Bobby's long, slender face. "Hiya John," he said, "how have you been?" his voice a pleasant melange of north Ontario and Back Bay Boston.

I asked, in turn, how he had been since our last meeting on that dark Sunday in Boston. "I'm taking it pretty easy," he said. "Some dinner appearances, like one here tonight. I'll be at the Stampede in July, then a little time at Banff. That's about it."

And then the new season would begin. How did Bobby Orr view that season as far as the Bruins were concerned?

"Well," he said, "we finished in first place last season, but we didn't play well in the playoffs and got our tails kicked in." He paused, then laughed, a self-conscious laugh. "Next season we will have essentially the same team so I think we can come back and be right up there again. But I'll tell you what we are going to have to do. We are going to have to give one hundred and ten percent next season because everyone else is going to be improved and they are going to be hot against us. They know we got beat. In order to repeat and end up in first place, we are all going to have to work like hell."

"What do you think are the Bruins' chances of breaking some of the scoring records the team set last season?"

"Well," he said, "I don't think we are going to be thinking about records. After what happened to us in the playoffs"— another low, grim laugh—"we are going to be thinking just about winning hockey games and trying to end up in first place. If the records come, fine, but I myself think they are going to be real, real tough to break." Again he laughed, but with more good humor in his voice.

I asked the question so many people had been asking since that seventh game: "What went wrong in the playoffs against Montreal?"

"Nothing went wrong," he said, annoyance in his voice. "We didn't play good hockey. We played terrible, every one of us. We just didn't play. We didn't skate, we didn't check, we did nothing at all. There were goals that we should have scored but didn't."

"But why didn't you play good hockey after playing so brilliantly all season long?"

"I don't know. I don't think anyone can explain something like that. It's like a slump in baseball or in any sport, it just happens."

"But wasn't the Montreal goaltender, Ken Dryden, a big factor?"

"Oh, no question," Bobby said, again with that hard laugh. "Oh, yes, you might indeed say he was very much a factor. Very, very much of a factor. We couldn't get the puck by him. He played well. But what you come down to is this: We played terrible. You can't take anything away from the Canadiens. They played real well. You know what they say: If you are playing poorly, the other team can make you play even more poorly."

"How do you think the loss will affect the team next season, Bobby?"

He stared for a moment out the window at the sunny street

below. "Well, it definitely is going to affect us, no doubt about that," he said. "It's going to affect us for the good. That's why I am saying we can come back to end up in first place again even though we are going to have to work harder than we did last season. But I think we will be willing to work harder because I think that loss will make us mad. Hell, it *should* make us mad."

"Then the fans should expect to see an even better Boston Bruin team in 1971–72 season," I said.

"I think we are going to be a more experienced team," he said. "I think we will be a wiser team."

"Wiser? In any particular way?"

"Wiser in that we know how close the difference is between winning and losing. We know we have a good hockey team and that we are going to win a lot of games. But now we know that we can't let up at any time against any team because we did and we got our tails kicked in."

"Was that, then, the lesson of the 1970–71 Stanley Cup playoffs as far as the Bruins were concerned?"

"Right," Bobby said. "We learned you just can't let up. We had been getting away with letting up some times during the season. But you can't do that. You have got to fight all the time. You can be ahead by four or five goals in hockey games today and lose. We found that out when we had Montreal on the run, 5–1, in that playoff game and they came back to beat us, what was it, 7–5?"

"Last year," I said, "was Tom Johnson's first as a head coach. Do you think that the team will be better now that he has had a year of coaching experience?"

"Oh, yes," Bobby said. "Tommy has been around the guys for a few years now, but last year was his first as the coach and now, I think, we all know each other better."

"Is there any area of the team that you think needs strengthening?"

"We could use strength in every area." Again that quick

laugh. "If we can get it."

"Who will be the tough teams for you in the East this season?"

"New York. Montreal. Toronto."

It was time for him to leave: first to a dinner later today, then to a summer of rest and the start of a new season—the 48th in the long history of those Big Bad Boston Bruins.

A Gallery of 1971-72 Action

Derek Sanderson, often called the best face-off man in hockey, swipes at the puck. Derek was one of the stars this season in a new movie titled "Face-Off," a full-length motion picture about hockey made in co-operation with the NHL. Film was the newest medium for Turk, who has already, at 25, written his life story and starred on his own television show.

Bobby Orr shows why he is idolized by fans and respected by the players as he dives to smother a shot, saving what seemed like a certain goal into the open net. Bobby also was still making those exciting forays into the other end of the ice. For most of the season he ranked among the NHL's top five scorers, battling Jean Ratelle for the lead in assists.

Phil Esposito proves for the puck with his stick as California's Carol Vadnais hurtles by him in this season's NHL All-Star game. Chicago's Bill White is blocked out of the play. Espy, who battled the Rangers' Jean Ratelle for the scoring title most of the season, rapped in the winning goal for the West in their 3-2 All-Star game victory.

Ted Green looks to pass the puck up to the front man, winger Ken Hodge. The record-busting Esposito-Hodge-Cashman line trailed the Rangers' Gag Line—Ratelle, Gilbert and Hadfield—in scoring this season, one reason being that opponents were putting out checking units against the Esposito line. Also, growls Esposito, "they're holding my stick."

Gerry Cheevers, eyes glittering behind the mask, moves to his left to close an opening as the Rangers' Bruce MacGregor drops the puck for a shot. This season coach Tom Johnson told people that his two goalkeepers, Gerry and Ed Johnston, "are playing as well as any two in the league." At one point Cheevers had a string of 15 games without a loss.

Johnny McKenzie, a challenging look on his face, tries to evade an official to land his fists on an opponent's face. In one game against the Rangers the pugnacious McKenzie smacked down one New Yorker after another, seeming to demoralize them. "We win when we hit and hit hard," McKenzie says. "We lose when we stop hitting. This year we won't stop hitting."

Eddie Westfall veers between two Flyers, eyes fixed on that alusive puck. All of the Bruins, said Phil Esposito, were thinking more of defense in this 1971-72 season. "The last man into the zone," he said, "is the first man back and sometimes it's even me." Then Espy added: "You play 78 games, right? The best team should surface. I think that team is us."

Bobby Orr cozies the puck to his stick while his off-season business partner, Mike Walton—they co-own a summer camp—glides to his side. A winger, Walton has also played center. Although he hadn't clocked a lot of ice-time by mid-season, Mike had scored 13 goals and 12 assists for 25 points, ninth highest on the team. Orr was second with 63 points.

Dallas Smith fights along the boards for the puck. Dallas, who has played so long in the shadow of fellow defenseman Bobby Orr, is beginning to receive recognition and was named to the East All-Star team. This season the Bruin defense tightened. Last year it yielded 2.6 goals a game; well into this season it was giving up only 2.1 per game.

BRUINS ALL-TIME RECORDS

Season	Won	Lost	Tied	Points	Goals For	Agst.	Position Finished
1924-25	6	24	0	12	49	119	Sixth (6)
1925-26	17	15	4	38	92	85	Fourth (7)
1926-27	21	20	3	45	97	89	Second (AD)
1927-28	20	13	11	51	77	70	First (AD)
1928-29	26	13	5	57	89	52	*First (AD)
1929-30	38	5	1	77	179	98	First (AD)
1930-31	28	10	6	62	143	90	First (AD)
1931-32	15	21	12	42	122	117	Fourth (AD)
1932-33	25	15	8	58	124	88	First (AD)
1933-34	18	25	5	41	111	130	Fourth (AD)
1934-35	26	16	6	58	129	112	First (AD)
1935-36	22	20	6	50	92	83	Second (AD)
1936-37	23	18	7	53	120	110	Second (AD)
1937-38	30	11	7	67	142	89	First (AD)
1938-39	36	10	2	74	156	76	*First (7)
1939-40	31	12	5	67	170	98	First (7)
1940-41	27	8	13	67	168	102	*First (7)
1941-42	25	17	6	56	160	118	Third (7)
1942-43	24	17	9	57	195	176	Second (6)
1943-44	19	26	5	43	223	268	Fifth (6)
1944-45	16	30	4	36	179	219	Fourth (6)
1945-46	24	18	8	56	167	156	Second (6)
1946-47	26	23	11	63	190	175	Third (6)
1947-48	23	24	13	59	167	168	Third (6)
1948-49	29	23	8	66	178	163	Second (6)
1949-50	22	32	16	60	198	228	Fifth (6)
1950-51	22	30	18	62	178	197	Fourth (6)
1951-52	25	29	16	66	162	176	Fourth (6)
1952-53	28	29	13	69	152	172	Third (6)
1953-54	32	28	10	74	177	181	Fourth (6)
1954-55	23	26	21	67	169	188	Fourth (6)
1955-56	23	34	13	59	147	185	Fifth (6)
1956-57	34	24	12	80	195	174	Third (6)
1957-58	27	28	15	69	199	194	Fourth (6)
1958-59	32	29	9	73	205	215	Second (6)
1959-60	28	34	8	64	220	241	Fifth (6)
1960-61	15	42	13	43	176	254	Sixth (6)
1961-62	15	47	8	38	177	306	Sixth (6)

1962-63	14	39	17	45	198	281	Sixth (6)
1963-64	18	40	12	48	170	212	Sixth (6)
1964-65	21	43	6	48	166	253	Sixth (6)
1965-66	21	43	6	48	174	275	Fifth (6)
1966-67	17	43	10	44	182	253	Sixth (6)
1967-68	37	27	10	84	259	215	Third (ED)
1968-69	42	18	16	100	303	221	Second (ED)
1969-70	40	17	19	99	277	216	*Second (ED)
1970-71	57	14	7	121	399	207	First (ED)

*Won Stanley Cup.   ( ) Teams in league.   (AD) American Division

(ED) Eastern Division

BRUINS STANLEY CUP RECORDS

Season	Opponent	Won	Lost	Tied	Goals For	Agst.	Winner
1924-25	Did not qualify						Victoria Cougars
1925-26	Did not qualify						Montreal Maroons
1926-27	Chicago	1	0	1	10	5	
	Rangers	1	0	1	3	1	
	Ottawa	0	2	2	3	7	Ottawa Senators
1927-28	Rangers	0	1	1	2	5	New York Rangers
1928-29	Canadiens	3	0	0	5	2	
	Rangers	2	0	0	4	1	BOSTON BRUINS
1929-30	Maroons	3	1	0	11	5	
	Canadiens	0	2	0	3	7	Montreal Canadiens
1930-31	Canadiens	2	3	0	13	13	Montreal Canadiens
1931-32	Did not qualify						Toronto Maple Leafs
1932-33	Toronto	2	3	0	7	9	New York Rangers
1933-34	Did not qualify						Chicago Black Hawks
1934-35	Toronto	1	3	0	2	7	Montreal Maroons
1935-36	Toronto	1	1	0	6	8	Detroit Red Wings
1936-37	Maroons	1	2	0	6	8	Detroit Red Wings
1937-38	Toronto	0	3	0	3	6	Chicago Black Hawks
1938-39	Rangers	4	3	0	14	12	
	Toronto	4	1	0	12	6	BOSTON BRUINS
1939-40	Rangers	2	4	0	9	15	New York Rangers
1940-41	Toronto	4	3	0	15	17	
	Detroit	4	0	0	12	6	BOSTON BRUINS
1941-42	Chicago	2	1	0	5	7	
	Detroit	0	2	0	5	9	Toronto Maple Leafs

1942-43	Canadiens	4	1	0	18	17	
	Detroit	0	4	0	5	16	Detroit Red Wings
1943-44	Did not qualify						Montreal Canadiens
1944-45	Detroit	3	4	0	22	22	Toronto Maple Leafs
1945-46	Detroit	4	1	0	16	10	
	Canadiens	1	4	0	13	19	Montreal Canadiens
1946-47	Canadiens	1	4	0	10	16	Toronto Maple Leafs
1947-48	Toronto	1	4	0	13	20	Toronto Maple Leafs
1948-49	Toronto	1	4	0	10	16	Toronto Maple Leafs
1949-50	Did not qualify						Detroit Red Wings
1950-51	Toronto	1	4	1	5	17	Toronto Maple Leafs
1951-52	Canadiens	3	4	0	12	18	Detroit Red Wings
1952-53	Detroit	4	2	0	21	21	
	Canadiens	1	4	0	9	16	Montreal Canadiens
1953-54	Canadiens	0	4	0	4	16	Detroit Red Wings
1954-55	Canadiens	1	4	0	9	16	Detroit Red Wings
1955-56	Did not qualify						Montreal Canadiens
1956-57	Detroit	4	1	0	15	14	
	Canadiens	1	4	0	6	15	Montreal Canadiens
1957-58	New York	4	2	0	28	16	
	Canadiens	2	4	0	14	16	Montreal Canadiens
1958-59	Toronto	3	4	0	21	20	Montreal Canadiens
1959-60	Did not qualify						Montreal Canadiens
1960-61	Did not qualify						Chicago Black Hawks
1961-62	Did not qualify						Toronto Maple Leafs
1962-63	Did not qualify						Toronto Maple Leafs
1963-64	Did not qualify						Toronto Maple Leafs
1964-65	Did not qualify						Montreal Canadiens
1965-66	Did not qualify						Montreal Canadiens
1966-67	Did not qualify						Toronto Maple Leafs
1967-68	Canadiens	0	4	0	8	15	Montreal Canadiens
1968-69	Toronto	4	0	0	24	5	
	Canadiens	2	4	0	16	15	Montreal Canadiens
1969-70	New York	4	2	0	25	16	
	Chicago	4	0	0	20	10	
	St. Louis	4	0	0	20	7	BOSTON BRUINS
1970-71	Canadiens	3	4	0	26	28	Montreal Canadiens
	TOTALS	97	112	6	540	573	

THE BRUINS' 1970-1971 RECORDS

NEW RECORD		OLD RECORD	
Most points, one season	BRUINS 121	103 MONTREAL	1968-69
Most wins, one season	BRUINS 57	46 MONTREAL	1968-69
Most road wins, one season	BRUINS 24	22 DETROIT, MONTREAL, (Twice Each)	
Most goals, one season	BRUINS 399	303 BRUINS	1968-69
Most home wins, one season	BRUINS 33	29 MONTREAL	1955-56
		BRUINS	1968-69

Most shorthanded goals, one season   14 CHICAGO   1964-65
BRUINS 25—(Westfall 7, Sanderson 6, Marcotte 6, Orr 3, D. Smith 2, Esposito 1)

Most assists one season,	BRUINS 695	497 BRUINS	1968-69

Most scoring points, one season   800 BRUINS   1968-69
BRUINS 1093

Most 20 goals or more scorers, one season
BRUINS 10—(Esposito, Orr, Bucyk, Hodge, Cashman, Stanfield, Sanderson, Westfall, McKenzie, Carleton)

Most 30 goals or more scorers,
one season BRUINS 5—(Esposito, Bucyk, Hodge, Orr, McKenzie)

Most 40 goals or more scorers,
one season BRUINS 3—(Esposito, Bucyk, Hodge)

Most 50 goals or more scorers, one
season BRUINS 2—(Esposito, Bucyk)

Fastest three goals, one team   21 Secs. CHICAGO   1952
BRUINS 20 Secs.—(Feb. 25 at Boston   (Bill Mosienko)
vs. Vancouver, 3rd pd., Bucyk, Westfall, Green) Bruins won 8-3

Most 100 point or more scorers, one
season BRUINS 4—(Esposito 152, Orr 139, Bucyk 116, Hodge 105)

First four scorers in scoring race
BRUINS—(Esposito 152, Orr 139, Bucyk 116, Hodge 105)

Most three goal games, one season
BRUINS 14—(Esposito 7, Bucyk 3, Westfall 1, McKenzie 2, Carleton 1)

INDIVIDUAL

Most three goal games, one season (Modern Era) 7—(Phil Esposito)	4 Beliveau, M. Richard, R. Hull, F. Mahovlich	
Most points one season (Phil Esposito) 152	126 Phil Esposito	1968-69
Most goals one season (Phil Esposito) 76	58 Bobby Hull, Chicago	1968-69
Most goals one season including playoffs 76—(Phil Esposito)	59 Jean Beliveau, Montreal	1955-56
Most assists, one season (Bobby Orr) 102	87 Bobby Orr, Bruins	1969-70

Most assists one season, including playoffs 102—(Bobby Orr)	98 Bobby Orr, Bruins	1969-70
Most goals one season by a defenseman 37—(Bobby Orr)	33 Bobby Orr, Bruins	1969-70
Most assists one season by a defenseman 102—(Bobby Orr)	87 Bobby Orr, Bruins	1969-70
Most points, one season, by a defenseman 139—(Bobby Orr)	120 Bobby Orr, Bruins	1969-70
Most goals one season by a center 76 (Phil Esposito)	49 Phil Esposito, Bruins	1968-69
Most assists one season by a left winger 65—(John Bucyk)	56 Bert Olmstead, Montreal	1955-56
Most assists one season by a right winger 62—(Ken Hodge)	59 Gordie Howe, Detroit	1968-69
Most points one season by a center 152 (Phil Esposito)	126 Phil Esposito, Bruins	1968-69
Most points one season by a left winger 116—(John Bucyk)	107 Bobby Hull, Chicago	1968-69
Most points one season by a right winger 105—(Ken Hodge)	103 Gordie Howe, Detroit	1968-69
Most power play goals one season 25 (Phil Esposito)	22 Bobby Hull, Chicago	1955-56
Most goals by a line one season 140 (Esposito 76, Hodge 43, Cashman 21)	114 Detroit (Howe, Mahovlich, Delvecchio)	1968-69
Most points by a line one season 336 (Esposito 152, Hodge 105, Cashman 79)	263 Bruins (Esposito, Hodge, Murphy) 1968-69	
Most shots one season 550 (Phil Esposito)		
Most consecutive 100 points or more season 2—(Bobby Orr)		
Most game winning goals 16 (Phil Esposito)		

LEADING BRUINS SCORERS

	POINTS	GOALS	ASSISTS	PENALTIES MINUTES
1924-25	22 J. Herberts	17 J. Herberts	5 J. Herberts	50 J. Herberts
1925-26	31 C. Cooper J. Herberts	28 C. Cooper	5 S. Cleghorn J. Herberts	70 L. Hitchman
1926-27	31 F. Fredrickson	18 F. Fredrickson H. Oliver	13 F. Fredrickson	130 E. Shore
1927-28	18 H. Oliver	13 H. Oliver	6 E. Shore	165 E. Shore
1928-29	23 H. Oliver	17 H. Oliver	8 W. Carson	96 E. Shore
1929-30	73 C. Weiland	43 C. Weiland	31 N. Gainor	105 E. Shore
1930-31	38 C. Weiland	25 C. Weiland	16 E. Shore	105 E. Shore
1931-32	39 A. Clapper	21 M. Barry	22 A. Clapper	80 E. Shore
1932-33	37 M. Barry	24 M. Barry	27 E. Shore	102 E. Shore

1933-34	39	M. Barry	27	M. Barry	17	N. Stewart	68	N. Stewart
1934-35	40	M. Barry	21	A. Clapper	26	E. Shore	80	A. Siebert
				N. Stewart				
1935-36	32	J. Beattie	14	J. Beattie	18	J. Beattie	66	A. Siebert
1936-37	35	W. Cowley	18	C. Sands	22	W. Cowley	94	A. Shields
1937-38	39	W. Cowley	20	R. Bauer	22	W. Cowley	54	W. Hollett
1938-39	42	W. Cowley	26	R. Conacher	34	W. Cowley	47	E. Shore
1939-40	52	M. Schmidt	22	M. Schmidt	30	M. Schmidt	55	J. Shewchuk
				W. Dumart				
1940-41	62	W. Cowley	24	R. Conacher	45	W. Cowley	61	D. Smith
1941-42	37	R. Conacher	24	R. Conacher	23	W. Cowley	70	D. Smith
1942-43	72	W. Cowley	27	W. Cowley	45	W. Cowley	67	M. Chamberlain
1943-44	82	H. Cain	36	H. Cain	46	H. Cain	75	P. Egan
1944-45	65	W. Cowley	32	H. Cain	40	W. Cowley	86	P. Egan
1945-46	40	D. Gallinger	22	W. Dumart	23	D. Gallinger	62	A. Guidolin
1946-47	62	M. Schmidt	30	R. Bauer	35	M. Schmidt	89	P. Egan
1947-48	40	G. Warwick	23	G. Warwick	23	K. Smith	81	P. Egan
				P. Babando				
1948-49	49	P. Ronty	22	J. Peirson	29	P. Ronty	92	P. Egan
				G. Warwick				
1949-50	59	P. Ronty	27	J. Peirson	36	P. Ronty	122	F. Flaman
1950-51	61	M. Schmidt	22	M. Schmidt	39	M. Schmidt	119	W. Ezinicki
1951-52	50	M. Schmidt	21	M. Schmidt	30	J. Peirson	127	W. Kyle
		J. Peirson						
1952-53	44	F. Mackell	27	F. Mackell	23	M. Schmidt	69	L. LaBine
1953-54	47	F. Mackell	21	J. Peirson	32	F. Mackell	81	R. Armstrong
		E. Sandford						
1954-55	42	L. LaBine	24	L. LaBine	24	F. Mackell	150	F. Flaman
		D. McKenney						
1955-56	37	V. Stasiuk	19	V. Stasiuk	24	D. McKenney	122	R. Armstrong
1956-57	60	D. McKenney	31	R. Chevrefils	39	D. McKenney	128	L. LaBine
1957-58	66	B. Horvath	30	B. Horvath	40	F. Mackell	72	F. Mackell
1958-59	62	D. McKenney	32	D. McKenney	36	J. Bucyk	101	F. Flaman
1959-60	80	B. Horvath	39	B. Horvath	49	D. McKenney	121	V. Stasiuk
1960-61	50	G. Toppazzini	26	D. McKenney	35	G. Toppazzini	95	J. Bartlett
1961-62	60	J. Bucyk	22	D. McKenney	40	J. Bucyk	116	T. Green
1962-63	66	J. Bucyk	27	J. Bucyk	40	M. Oliver	117	T. Green
1963-64	68	M. Oliver	24	M. Oliver	44	M. Oliver	145	T. Green
1964-65	55	J. Bucyk	26	J. Bucyk	29	J. Bucyk	156	T. Green
1965-66	60	M. Oliver	27	J. Bucyk	42	M. Oliver	113	T. Green
1966-67	48	J. Bucyk	20	H. Martin	30	J. Bucyk	112	G. Marotte
1967-68	84	P. Esposito	35	P. Esposito	49	P. Esposito	150	D. Awrey
1968-69	126	P. Esposito	49	P. Esposito	77	P. Esposito	146	D. Sanderson
1969-70	120	R. Orr	43	P. Esposito	87	R. Orr	125	R. Orr
1970-71	152	P. Esposito	76	P. Esposito	102	R. Orr	141	D. Awrey

BRUINS TROPHY WINNERS

Georges Vezina Trophy—for goaltender with best record:
    1929-30 Cecil (Tiny) Thompson
    1932-33 Cecil (Tiny) Thompson
    1935-36 Cecil (Tiny) Thompson

1937-38 Cecil (Tiny) Thompson
1938-39 Frank Brimsek
1941-42 Frank Brimsek

Dr. David A. Hart Trophy—for most valuable player:
1932-33 Eddie Shore; 1934-35 Eddie Shore
1935-36 Eddie Shore; 1937-38 Eddie Shore
1940-41 Bill Cowley; 1942-43 Bill Cowley
1950-51 Milton Schmidt
1968-69 Phil Esposito
1969-70 Bobby Orr
1970-71 Bobby Orr

Lady Byng Trophy—for most gentlemanly player:
1939-40 Bobby Bauer; 1940-41 Bobby Bauer
1946-47 Bobby Bauer
1959-60 Don McKenney
1970-71 John Bucyk

Calder Trophy—for outstanding rookie:
1938-39 Frank Brimsek; 1949-50 Jack Gelineau
1956-57 Larry Regan
1966-67 Bobby Orr
1967-68 Derek Sanderson

James Norris Memorial Trophy—for outstanding defenseman:
1967-68 Bobby Orr
1968-69 Bobby Orr
1969-70 Bobby Orr
1970-71 Bobby Orr

Art Ross Trophy—for scoring leader:
1968-69 Phil Esposito
1969-70 Bobby Orr
1970-71 Phil Esposito

Conn Smythe Trophy—most valuable player to team in playoffs:
1969-70 Bobby Orr

ELIZABETH C. DUFRESNE TROPHY

"To the Boston player who has been most outstanding in home games."

1935-36 Tiny Thompson	1941-42 Milt Schmidt	1945-46 Jack Crawford
1936-37 Eddie Shore	Woody Dumart	1946-47 Milt Schmidt
1937-38 Eddie Shore	Bobby Bauer	1947-48 Frank Brimsek
1938-39 Eddie Shore	1942-43 Frank Brimsek	1948-49 Pat Egan
1939-40 Dit Clapper	1943-44 Bill Cowley	1949-50 Milt Schmidt
1940-41 Dit Clapper	1944-45 Jack Crawford	1950-51 Milt Schmidt

1951-52 Jim Henry	1958-59 Vic Stasiuk	1965-66 John Bucyk
1952-53 Flem Mackell	1959-60 Bronco Horvath	1966-67 Bobby Orr
1953-54 Jim Henry	1960-61 Leo Boivin	1967-68 Phil Esposito
1954-55 Leo LaBine	1961-62 Doug Mohns	1968-69 Phil Esposito
1955-56 Terry Sawchuk	1962-63 John Bucyk	1969-70 Bobby Orr
1956-57 Jerry Toppazzini	1963-64 Ed Johnston	1970-71 Phil Esposito
1957-58 Jerry Toppazzini	1964-65 Ted Green	

BRUINS ALL STARS

The following Bruins have been named through the years on the National Hockey League All-Star Team. (The league did not recognize All-Star teams until the 1930-31 season.)

FRANK BRIMSEK
1939 ★ 1942

DIT CLAPPER
1939 ★ 1940 ★ 1941

BILL COWLEY
1938 ★ 1941 ★ 1943

JOHN CRAWFORD
★ 1946 ★

FLEMING MACKELL
★ 1953 ★

BILL QUACKENBUSH
★ 1951 ★

MILT SCHMIDT
1939 ★ 1947 ★ 1951

BABE SIEBERT
★ 1936 ★

EDDIE SHORE
1931 ★ 1932 ★ 1933 ★ 1935
1936 ★ 1938 ★ 1939

TINY THOMPSON
1936 ★ 1938

BOBBY ORR
1968 ★ 1969 ★ 1970 ★ 1971

PHIL ESPOSITO
1969 ★ 1970 ★ 1971

ART ROSS (Coach)
★ 1939 ★

RALPH WEILAND (Coach)
★ 1941 ★

JOHN BUCYK
★ 1971 ★

KEN HODGE
★ 1971 ★